D1149280

LIFE SKILLS

225

Ready-to-Use Health Activities for Success and Well-Being (Grades 6–12)

SANDRA McTAVISH

JOSSEY-BASS™
An Imprint of
Ⓦ**WILEY**

Library of Congress Cataloging-in-Publication Data
McTavish, Sandra.
  Life skills : 225 ready-to-use health activities for success and
well-being (grades 6-12) / Sandra McTavish.— 1st ed.
       p. cm.
Summary: Provides worksheets with exercises on such health topics as
drugs, alcohol, and smoking; sex; love, marriage, and family
relationships; life skills; stress; food-related issues; body and body
image; and self-esteem.
  ISBN 978-0-7879-6959-2 (pbk)
1. Health education—Juvenile literature. 2. Teenagers—Health and
hygiene—Juvenile literature. 3. Life skills—Study and
teaching—Activity programs—Juvenile literature. [1. Teenagers—Health
and hygiene. 2. Life skills.] I. Title.
  LB1587.A3M38 2003
  613'.0433—dc22
                              2003018303

FIRST EDITION
PB Printing 10

ACKNOWLEDGMENTS

Although only one name appears on the front cover, many people contributed hours of their time to bring this book to the published form. Without them, this book would still be an idea floating in my head.

I want to thank and dedicate this book to these people: to Paul Foster at Jossey-Bass for believing in my idea; to Steve Thompson and the others at Jossey-Bass who spent many hours transforming the manuscript into a book, including Elisa Rassen, Pamela Berkman, and Sandra Beris; to my parents who read every word on every page, gave me lots of editorial advice, and cheered me on; to Steve Salt who did all the graphics; to the experts in the various fields who read over certain chapters and provided advice: Drs. Bill and Barbara Coon (Chapter One), Dr. David Mathies (Chapters Two and Seven), Lynn Newell (Chapters Three and Five), Jeff Klink (Chapters Four and Eight), Andrea Horcsok (Chapter Six); to my former colleagues in the Southwood Secondary School Physical Education Department—Rob Baird, Cindy Clipper, Sandy Fallis, John Genovese, Marg Procter, Jason Renfrew, Lara Shantz, Brad Sims, and Barb Wilson—who inspired many of these worksheets and were a big part of the reason why I loved teaching phys. ed.; to all my former students who completed many of these worksheets and tested this material without realizing they were testing it, and were the other big reason why I loved teaching phys. ed.; to Colleen Gray, who helped inspire some of these worksheets; to my brothers, Todd and Ian, and my sister, Marni, for their support; and last (but not least), to Doug for his kindness, support, and friendship.

Thanks to all of you.

Sandra McTavish

ABOUT THE AUTHOR

Sandra McTavish began her teaching career in 1995 as a full-time member of the physical education department of Centennial Collegiate in Guelph, Ontario. She then transferred to Southwood Secondary School in Cambridge, Ontario, where she taught a full-credit health course along with a course that combined aerobics and health education. She left teaching in 2000 when she was hired by the Ontario government to work on the new provincial-wide literacy test. She has remained in Toronto writing educational resource material since then, while also teaching part-time at Humber College. As a physical education teacher, Ms. McTavish has coached boys' volleyball and girls' gymnastics. She is the author of *Ready . . . Set . . . English!* (Jossey-Bass, 2002) and has contributed to the magazine *Physical Education Digest.*

ABOUT THIS BOOK

This resource book consists of 225 ready-to-use one-page worksheets that cover a variety of health topics in a variety of manners. The worksheets are divided into the following eight sections, or chapters:

Section 1: Drugs, Alcohol, and Smoking

This chapter, which includes 31 worksheets, begins with a few inviting introductory activities, such as *Word Association,* where students name the words they think of when they see the words *alcohol, drugs,* and *cigarettes.* It then focuses on issues related to smoking, with worksheets that examine trends in smoking, secondhand smoke, reasons why people smoke, and ways to help smokers quit. Next, the chapter focuses on drugs. These worksheets classify the different types of drugs and examine facts about drug use. The last worksheets take a look at the use and abuse of alcohol, the effects of drinking, and reasons why people start drinking, and cover such issues as alcoholism, fetal alcohol syndrome, and drinking and driving.

Section 2: Sex and Sex-Related Issues

This chapter, consisting of 32 worksheets, discusses female and male sexual organs, reasons why people have sex, and facts and myths about sex. The chapter then focuses on birth control with worksheets like *Dr. Birth Control,* in which students have to determine the birth control method they would suggest for various couples. Later worksheets look at options and issues people have to face with pregnancy. Finally, this chapter examines sexually transmitted infections (STIs), homosexuality, infertility options and adoption, sexual harassment, and date rape. The chapter closes with a few fun worksheets—for example, *Sex Jeopardy,* which tests students' knowledge about all the issues covered in the chapter, and the vocabulary game *Alphabet Soup.*

Section 3: Love, Relationships, Marriage, and Family

The 31 worksheets in this chapter examine friendship and romantic relationships. The chapter begins by having students analyze their friendships and how their friends play different roles in their lives. A few worksheets examine the negative aspects of cliques. Next, the exercises allow students to explore dating and romantic relationships. Students reflect on the differences between love and infatuation, Robert Sternberg's love triangle, and the qualities they might seek in an ideal mate. Following this, the subject shifts, and the worksheets examine marriage and family issues. The students have an opportunity to write their own marriage vows, examine ideal marriages and think about what makes them work, and explore problems some marriages encounter and why some end. The chapter looks at Jay Haley's family life cycle as well as the challenges faced by nontraditional families.

Section 4: Life Skills

The 29 worksheets in this chapter explore various life skills students need in order to cope in the adult world. Starting with Maslow's Hierarchy of Needs, the students look at the difference between high and low self-esteem, give some thought to their goals in 5, 10, and 20 years, and learn about assertive behavior, how to deal with difficult people, and conflict resolution. They also examine what makes a good leader, effective communication and time management skills, and the problems of violence.

Section 5: Stress

This chapter includes 23 worksheets. The first set of worksheets helps students identify what makes them stressed. Then, the chapter focuses on various reactions to stress and coping mechanisms for dealing with it. The chapter concludes with worksheets covering the painful issues of suicide, death, and dying.

Section 6: Food and Food-Related Issues

With the help of the 27 worksheets in this chapter, students reflect on their eating habits and ways they might improve these habits. They fill in the USDA's food pyramid. There are individual worksheets on topics including calories, water, vitamins, cholesterol, protein, carbohydrates, fiber, fat, and additives. And there are a few fun worksheets here, too, like the one titled *Just Because It's a Salad Doesn't Mean It's Healthy,* in which students analyze what makes three salads unhealthy and how they could change the ingredients to make them healthier. The chapter ends with a few worksheets on eating disorders.

Section 7: Your Body and Body Image

This chapter, with 26 worksheets, begins by examining students' thoughts about their own body image and body type. After that, fun worksheets let students learn the function of different organs, body parts, and body systems, as well as anatomical terminology. Later worksheets focus on the different types of medical specialties, the difference between a virus and bacteria, and basic first aid. Students get an opportunity to diagnose an emergency and deal with the problem. Finally, students examine their fitness habits, the difference between anaerobic and aerobic energy, four components of fitness, and delayed onset muscle soreness.

Section 8: Self-Esteem and Knowing Yourself

While the previous chapter encourages students to feel good about their physical self, this chapter stresses the need to feel good about their personality. In these 26 worksheets, students look at what their names may mean for them, their favorite things, their handwriting, their personality type, how their birth order may have affected their personality, their highs and lows, the five senses, and so on, as they examine what makes each individual unique.

At the end of the book is an answer key section providing answers as well as suggested responses. There is also a bibliography that highlights the books and resources used during the research for this book.

This is a helpful, fun, and easy-to-use resource. So, let's get started!

CONTENTS

SECTION 1

DRUGS, ALCOHOL, AND SMOKING

Contents

SECTION **2**

SEX AND SEX-RELATED ISSUES

SECTION **3**

LOVE, RELATIONSHIPS, MARRIAGE, AND FAMILY

SECTION **4**

LIFE SKILLS

Contents

SECTION **5**

STRESS

SECTION **6**

FOOD AND FOOD-RELATED ISSUES

SECTION **7**

YOUR BODY AND BODY IMAGE

SECTION **8**

SELF-ESTEEM AND KNOWING YOURSELF

Contents

DRUGS, ALCOHOL, AND SMOKING

Of all the tyrannies which have usurped power over humanity,
few have been able to enslave the mind and body
as imperiously as drug addiction.

Freda Adler

NAME _____   DATE

Word Association

What do you think of when you see the word . . . ?

Instructions: Write in the smaller circles the words that you associate with the words that are shown in the larger circles.

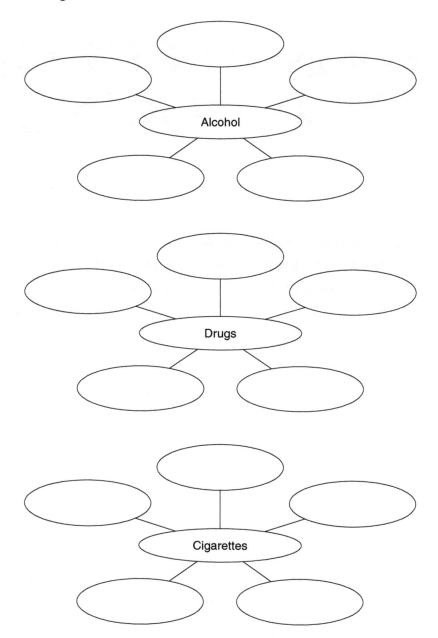

How many of these words do you consider to be positive (mark these with a +) and how many do you consider negative (mark these with a −)?

NAME _____   DATE

What Drug Am I?

Read each riddle and guess the name of the drug the riddle describes.

1. Some call me weed.
   Some call me pot.
   Some smoke me in a joint
   And think they're really hot.

What drug am I? _____

2. Even though teens drink me
   They should be twenty-one
   If they want me legally
   For their parties and their fun.

What drug am I? _____

3. There's no penalty to smoke me.
   Some people have a fit.
   They try to stop this addiction,
   But they just can't quit.

What drug am I? _____

4. People snort it up their nose
   And call it coke or snow or ice.
   It's highly addictive; don't try it
   If you want some good advice.

What drug am I? _____

5. I'm very, very popular
   And found in coffee and tea.
   I'm not illegal anywhere
   And people drink me.

What drug am I? _____

Trends in Tobacco Use

Circle the correct answer. (The source for the information in this quiz is the American Lung Association.)

1. What percentage of Americans die each year from smoking-related illnesses?
   a. 5 percent
   b. 10 percent
   c. 20 percent
   d. 50 percent

2. According to a recent survey, what percentage of the American population smokes cigarettes regularly?
   a. 5 percent
   b. 15 percent
   c. 25 percent
   d. 45 percent

3. According to statistics, which state has the highest percentage of smokers?
   a. Alaska
   b. California
   c. Florida
   d. Nevada

4. According to statistics, which state has the lowest percentage of smokers?
   a. California
   b. Texas
   c. Utah
   d. Washington

5. What percentage of smokers want to quit smoking?
   a. 25 percent
   b. 50 percent
   c. 70 percent
   d. 95 percent

6. Of those who want to quit smoking, what percentage of people actually attempt to quit each year?
   a. 15 percent
   b. 35 percent
   c. 50 percent
   d. 75 percent

7. Of the people who attempt to quit each year, what percentage of them are actually successful in quitting?
   a. 2.5 percent
   b. 10 percent
   c. 20 percent
   d. 50 percent

8. Which age group has the highest population of smokers in the United States?
   a. 18- to 24-year-olds
   b. 30- to 34-year-olds
   c. 45- to 54-year-olds
   d. 70- to 85-year-olds

Time Line: A Short History of Tobacco and Cigarette Use

Here is a list of highlights in the history of tobacco and cigarette use. Arrange the events in the order in which they occurred by placing the number of the event on the time line below. The first one is done for you.

1. A twenty-two-year-old named James A. Bonsack of Virginia invented the world's first cigarette-making machine, which rolled up to 120,000 cigarettes a day.

2. Jean Nicot (the word *nicotine* comes from his name), French ambassador to Portugal, shipped tobacco plants to the queen of France so that she could grow them in her herb garden.

3. This was the last time the *Journal of the American Medical Association* reported that tobacco did not cause health problems.

4. The British settlers who founded Jamestown (the first New World colony) sent the first tobacco shipment from America to England. The shipment sold quickly, and as a result tobacco became an important export for the colonists.

5. President John F. Kennedy requested a report on smoking and health from the U.S. Surgeon General. The report, which took two years to complete, stated that smoking caused lung cancer and other diseases.

6. Antismoking leader Lucy Page Gaston founded the Chicago Anti-Cigarette League of America and helped push through antismoking bills.

7. Christopher Columbus landed in San Salvador, hoping to find gold. Instead of gold, the natives gave him tobacco, which Columbus thought was useless and threw away.

8. The Federal Trade Commission banned tobacco companies from using ads that claimed smoking provided health benefits.

9. Spanish and Portuguese explorers became addicted to tobacco and brought this habit home with them. Soon people from every nation in Europe smoked or chewed tobacco.

Least
Recent   <u>7</u>   ____   ____   ____   ____   ____   ____   ____   ____   Most
                                                                                       Recent

Thoughts About Secondhand Smoke

What is secondhand smoke? _____
_____

Why is secondhand smoke dangerous?

_____

_____

For each statement listed below, decide whether you agree, disagree, or are undecided. Then, in the comment section, explain your position.

1. Smokers should not be allowed to smoke in any restaurants, bars, or public places in the United States.

	Agree		Disagree		Undecided

Comments: _____

_____

_____

2. Smokers who have children should not be allowed to smoke in the home or near their children.

	Agree		Disagree		Undecided

Comments: _____

_____

_____

3. Since it has been proven that secondhand smoke is so lethal, a law should be passed making cigarette smoking illegal.

	Agree		Disagree		Undecided

Comments: _____

_____

_____

Young Kids and Smoking

Kids begin smoking as early as nine and ten years of age. By the time they reach high school, many of these smokers are addicted. In fact, a National Youth Tobacco Survey reported that over 25 percent of ninth graders smoke regularly.

With all the information and statistics that prove smoking is harmful, why do kids start smoking in the first place? Think of five reasons why they do.

1. _____

2. _____

3. _____

4. _____

5. _____

Imagine that you have been hired by the American Lung Association to encourage young smokers to stop smoking or to avoid trying smoking in the first place. List ten things you would do in a campaign to persuade the youth of today not to smoke.

1. _____

2. _____

3. _____

4. _____

5. _____

6. _____

7. _____

8. _____

9. _____

10. _____

Show Me the Money

The main reason people should not smoke is obvious: their health. However, another good reason for not smoking is financial. The objective of this worksheet is to show how much money a smoker could save by not buying cigarettes.

Today, a pack of cigarettes costs approximately $5.00. Imagine that you are a smoker who smokes an average of one pack of cigarettes a day.

In order to see how much money you might save in one year by not buying cigarettes, multiply the price of one pack of cigarettes (that is, $5.00) by 365 = _____ (a).

If you did not spend this money on cigarettes, you could have invested it in the bank. Imagine that you did invest the money in the bank at an interest rate of 5 percent. To determine how much you made on the interest, multiply your total from (a) by .05 = _____ (b).

Then add the number from (a) to the number from (b) to see how much money you could have saved in a year. That total is _____ (c).

In order to see approximately how much you could have saved by not spending money on cigarettes for 5 years, multiply the amount from (c) by 5. That total is _____ (d).

In order to see approximately how much you could have saved by not spending money on cigarettes for 10 years, multiply the amount from (c) by 10. That total is _____ (e).

In order to see approximately how much you could have saved by not spending money on cigarettes for 20 years, multiply the amount from (c) by 20. That total is _____ (f).

In order to see approximately how much you could have saved by not spending money on cigarettes for 40 years, multiply the amount from (c) by 40. That total is _____ (g).

Think how much a 40-year smoker spends on cigarettes. What might you do with that money instead of spending it on cigarettes? Answer this question on the back of this sheet.

Getting Tough on Smoking: An Editorial

Read the editorial below and answer the questions that follow on a separate piece of paper.

In the last few years, the number of young people taking up smoking has increased. Most nonsmokers, and even some smokers, are horrified by the statistics. Everyone complains and points fingers, but few people propose ways of dealing with the problem. However, I'm going to change all that with my ideas on how to stop kids from taking up this nasty habit.

First, Hollywood needs to BUTT OUT! By that I mean a law is needed to ban Hollywood from showing actors smoking. Let's face it, kids idolize actors, and when they see a star smoking, they think it's cool and OK to smoke. We can eliminate this message by eliminating smoking in films.

Next, laws need to change so that people who are ill with smoking-related diseases must pay all their medical expenses, even if they are covered by health insurance. The law should state that health insurance will not cover a penny if the ill person smokes. This may seem harsh, but this stiff financial penalty may cause a lot of young people to really think twice before lighting up their first cigarette.

Finally, all fourth- or fifth-grade students should have to participate in a mandatory class trip to a local hospital to visit people who are dying from smoking-related illnesses. This, too, may seem horrific and extreme, but if the horror of seeing a person dying because of smoking causes even one kid not to start smoking, then the whole experience is worthwhile.

Although I have many more ideas, I believe these three suggestions, if acted upon, are all that is needed for our nation to force our young people to think twice before starting a deadly habit.

1. Summarize the three ideas that the author proposes to get kids to stop smoking or not start in the first place.

2. For each method, explain why or why not you think this would be successful.

3. What three additional ideas can you suggest that might stop young people from smoking? Write an editorial like this one in which you explain your thoughts.

Antismoking Slogans

Imagine that you work for an advertising agency that has been hired to create an antismoking campaign. Rather than create a brand-new slogan, you've decided to rework a slogan for another product and turn it into a nonsmoking slogan. For example, one of your ideas is to take Nike's "Just do it" slogan and reword it so that it reads: "Smoking: Just don't do it." You've been asked to come up with eight ideas. Below are some popular slogans. For each slogan, reword it so that it becomes an antismoking slogan or an encouragement-to-quit slogan. With your new slogan, people should be able to figure out the original slogan. Try not to alter the wording of the original too much.

1. American Express credit cards: "Don't leave home without it."

   _____

2. Calvin Klein jeans: "Nothing comes between me and my Calvins."

   _____

3. Club Med resorts: "Vacation is a world where there are no locks on the doors, or the mind or the body."

   _____

4. Coldene cold tablets: "Don't spread the cold. . . . Spread the word."

   _____

5. Florida Citrus Commission: "A day without orange juice is like a day without sunshine."

   _____

6. Rolaids antacid tablets: "How do you spell relief? R-O-L-A-I-D-S."

   _____

7. Pepsodent toothpaste: "You'll wonder where the yellow went when you brush your teeth with Pepsodent."

   _____

8. Pampers diapers: "Give your baby something you never had as a baby: a drier bottom."

   _____

You Be the Judge

Janice Henderson was born in the 1950s and began smoking in sixth grade. Both of her parents smoked. In fact, almost everyone Janice knew when she was growing up smoked. Janice tried to quit when she was in her early twenties but was too addicted. Today, Janice is dying of lung cancer. She is suing the tobacco companies for $25 million because she believes that the cigarette companies did not sufficiently warn her about the addictive quality and harm of smoking. In the space provided, write down your thoughts about this case. Do you think Janice should win her case? Why or why not?

_____

_____

_____

_____

_____

_____

_____

_____

_____

_____

_____

_____

_____

_____

_____

NAME _____   DATE _____

Classifying the Types of Drugs

Drugs can be classified into various categories. Four of the main categories are these:

1. *Stimulants:* These drugs act on the central nervous system and increase brain activity.

2. *Depressants:* These are the opposite of stimulants. They act on the central nervous system and slow down brain activity.

3. *Hallucinogens:* These drugs distort the user's senses and ability to perceive reality.

4. *Narcotics:* These drugs reduce pain and induce sleep.

Complete the following chart by putting the name of all the drugs found below it into their appropriate category.

Stimulants	Depressants	Hallucinogens	Narcotics

codeine	cocaine	morphine
alcohol	LSD	nicotine
marijuana	heroin	tranquilizers
caffeine	barbiturates	PCP (also known
methadone	crack	as angel dust)

Copyright © 2004 by John Wiley & Sons, Inc.

The Types-of-Drugs Chart

This chart is incomplete. Fill in the missing sections with the proper information.

	Depressants	Hallucinogens	Narcotics	Stimulants
What this type of drug does		These drugs distort the user's senses and ability to perceive reality.	These drugs reduce pain and induce sleep.	
Example of drugs in this category	alcohol tranquilizers barbiturates			cocaine caffeine nicotine crack
How the drugs enter the body				swallowed snorted injected
Medical uses of this type of drug			Used for pain relief	

Facts and Myths on Drug Use

Here is a list of statements about drugs that are based on facts or myths. If you think the statement is true, circle the word FACT. If you think the statement is false, circle the word MYTH.

1. FACT or MYTH: One drink of alcohol will not affect a person's driving.

2. FACT or MYTH: Brain damage can occur if a person drinks heavily over a long period of time.

3. FACT or MYTH: All alcoholics live on the streets, beg for money, and talk to themselves.

4. FACT or MYTH: People can become addicted to prescription drugs.

5. FACT or MYTH: Not all drugs are harmful.

6. FACT or MYTH: Drinking hard liquor will make you more drunk than drinking beer or wine.

7. FACT or MYTH: Smoking cigarettes is more addictive than chewing tobacco.

8. FACT or MYTH: If the mother breathes in secondhand smoke, it can harm her unborn baby.

9. FACT or MYTH: Teenagers who have a parent who smokes are more likely to start smoking than teenagers whose parents do not smoke.

10. FACT or MYTH: Cigarettes are just as harmful as marijuana.

11. FACT or MYTH: Smoking can stunt a person's growth.

12. FACT or MYTH: You'll be able to handle drugs better the more you use them.

13. FACT or MYTH: Having a shower will sober up a person.

14. FACT or MYTH: If the mother drinks alcohol, it can harm her unborn baby.

15. FACT or MYTH: People who use drugs regularly may suffer from depression.

16. FACT or MYTH: People who smoke regularly have difficulty quitting.

Time Line: History of Drug Regulations in the United States

Here is a list of significant events in the history of drug regulations in the United States. Arrange the regulations in the order in which they occurred by placing the number of the event on the time line below. The first one is done for you.

1. The Food, Drug, and Cosmetic Act was passed; this meant that a company had to submit a new drug application to the FDA (Food and Drug Administration) before it was deemed safe for public use.

2. The Orphan Drug Act, which gave tax incentives to drug companies that were developing new drugs for rare disorders, was a positive advancement in discovering drugs that could treat rare diseases.

3. The Harrison Narcotic Act was the first law passed in the United States to regulate the sale of narcotic drugs and cocaine.

4. A federal act was signed that permitted only American citizens to import opium into the United States.

5. With the Controlled Substance Act, all controlled substances were placed in one of five schedules or categories depending on dependency or medical use.

6. The Pure Food and Drug Act required the accurate labeling of food and drugs.

7. A constitutional amendment was introduced that prohibited the sale of alcoholic beverages. (This was known to many as Prohibition.)

Least
Recent   __4__ ____ ____ ____ ____ ____ ____   Most
Recent

NAME   DATE

Drug Use and Different Ages

The chart below, taken from the National Institute on Drug Abuse, examines the most commonly used drugs among different age groups.

Read the chart and then complete the questions that follow.

Drug	Ages 12-17	Ages 18-25	Ages 26-34	Ages 35+
Alcohol	21%	61%	63%	53%
Cigarettes	20%	35%	35%	27%
Marijuana	8%	12%	7%	2%
Cocaine	0.4%	1.3%	1.2%	0.4%

1. According to this chart, which two age groups have the highest percentages of reported drug use?

   _____

2. Why do you think these age groups have a higher use than the other two age groups?

   _____

   _____

   _____

   _____

3. What drug has the highest percentage of use and what drug has the lowest percentage of use?

   _____

4. Why do you think the drug with the lowest percentage of use is not so popular a choice as the drug with the highest percentage?

   _____

   _____

   _____

   _____

The Drug-Use Continuum

Here is a description of drug users based on the drug use continuum.

- *Nonuser:* Has never used a drug.
- *Experimental user:* Has tried a drug once or several times.
- *Occasional user:* Uses a drug (or drugs) frequently on special occasions or when the opportunity presents itself.
- *Regular user:* Has a predictable pattern of use and seeks opportunities to use the drug.
- *Dependent user:* Uses drugs regularly, predictably, and frequently and depends on the drugs in order to function.

Note that a dependent user would have started as a nonuser and then worked up the continuum.

Write the names of the following five people on the continuum chart below.

1. Carlitos wakes up every Saturday morning and smokes three marijuana joints. He doesn't do this during the week because it would affect his performance at work.

2. At a party, Daoud, a member of his high school rugby team, is offered a marijuana joint. He refuses. He's never taken any drugs before because he wants to keep his body clean for sports.

3. Alexa never had a drink of alcohol until she went to Lewis's party. Then she tried beer for the first time.

4. Oliver is a manager at a bank; however, he may soon lose his job because of his drinking habits. He drinks as soon as he gets up, at lunchtime, during dinner, and before bed.

5. Candace is going to a party next weekend. Ken always has Ecstasy at his parties and Candace usually gets high on it when she's there. She doesn't get high any other time.

Nonuser	Experimental User	Occasional User	Regular User	Dependent User
_____	_____	_____	_____	_____

The Marijuana Expert

A nightly news program is doing a special on marijuana use among teens. You work for the National Institutes of Health and are being interviewed on the show as a medical expert on marijuana use and its effects. Here are some questions that you will be asked. Write your response to each question in the space provided.

1. How do people use marijuana?

   _____

   _____

2. Why do teens use marijuana?

   _____

   _____

3. What are the immediate effects of using marijuana?

   _____

   _____

4. What are the long-term effects of using marijuana?

   _____

   _____

5. What does the term *gateway drug* mean, and why do some people consider marijuana to be one?

   _____

   _____

6. What are the signs that a person has used marijuana?

   _____

   _____

7. Where can someone who is addicted to marijuana go for help?

   _____

   _____

18

To Legalize or Not to Legalize?

At the present time, it is illegal to smoke or use marijuana in the United States. Imagine that a group is suing the government in the hopes of changing the law and making marijuana legal.

If you were the lawyer defending the group that wants to legalize marijuana use, what arguments would you make?

_____

_____

_____

_____

_____

_____

_____

If you were the lawyer defending the government that does not want the law changed, what arguments would you use?

_____

_____

_____

_____

_____

_____

_____

_____

A Venn Diagram Comparing Tobacco and Marijuana

Tobacco and marijuana are similar yet different. Use the Venn diagram below to write in point form the similarities and differences between these two drugs. In the space where the two circles meet, write the similarities. Where they don't join, write the differences.

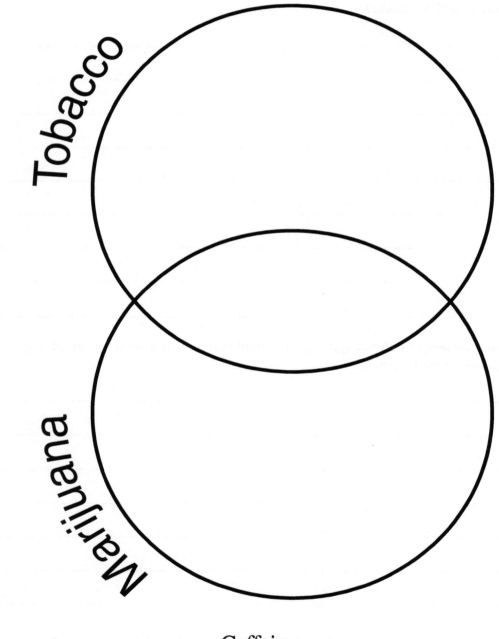

Tobacco

Marijuana

Caffeine

NAME DATE

Caffeine

Caffeine is the world's most popular drug. Although many people deny it, caffeine is addictive. People who have lots of caffeine in their daily diet and then suddenly lower their caffeine intake usually experience symptoms of withdrawal. Below is a list of products that contain caffeine. Rank the products according to their caffeine content: 1 has the most caffeine; 13 has the least. You may find some surprises when you learn the answers.

_____ One 1-ounce piece of milk chocolate

_____ One can of Pepsi

_____ One can of Coke or Diet Coke

_____ One 2-ounce serving of espresso

_____ One 12-ounce glass of iced tea

_____ One can of Mountain Dew

_____ One 7-ounce cup of automatic drip coffee

_____ One cup of instant decaffeinated coffee

_____ One cup of imported, brewed tea

_____ One can of Jolt cola

_____ One Anacin tablet

_____ One can of Dr. Pepper

_____ One cup of hot cocoa

NAME _____   DATE _____

The Truth About Anabolic Steroids

Answer true or false to the following statements about anabolic steroids.

1. TRUE or FALSE: Anabolic steroids are used illegally by some athletes to enhance and improve their performance.

2. TRUE or FALSE: Anabolic steroids may cause women's voices to deepen and more facial and body hair to grow.

3. TRUE or FALSE: Anabolic steroids increase men's sperm count, sexual desire, and sexual performance.

4. TRUE or FALSE: Anabolic steroids may be prescribed by a doctor for people suffering from testosterone deficiency, postmenopausal osteoporosis, and other illnesses.

5. TRUE or FALSE: Athletes taking anabolic steroids do not have to work out longer and harder to see a desired effect than they would without the steroids.

6. TRUE or FALSE: Anabolic steroids come from a chemical derivative of the male sex hormone.

7. TRUE or FALSE: Anabolic steroids may cause acne, liver damage, and uncontrollable aggression in both men and women.

8. TRUE or FALSE: No one can purchase anabolic steroids legally.

9. TRUE or FALSE: Most athletes who take anabolic steroids illegally take 10 to 100 times the normal dosage prescribed for humans.

Tic-Tac Drugs: Teacher Page

This activity requires students to work in pairs. Give each pair a copy of the student page of this exercise (following); let each pair decide who is PLAYER 1 and who is PLAYER 2. Read the first question aloud for PLAYER 1. PLAYER 1 writes his or her answer on the student page after "Answer to Question 1." After all the PLAYER 1's in the class have finished writing down their answer, give them the correct answer. If PLAYER 1 is correct, he or she can put an X anywhere in the tic-tac-toe grid. If PLAYER 1 is incorrect, then PLAYER 2 can put an O anywhere in the tic-tac-toe grid. Then, ask the next question of PLAYER 2. Follow this same procedure until all the students have completed the game.

Nine questions are provided per game. You have been provided with two sets of nine questions so that your students can play two games.

Questions for Game 1

PLAYER 1'S QUESTION: Can marijuana be eaten? Answer: Yes.

PLAYER 2'S QUESTION: Can inhalants enter the body by being smoked? Answer: No.

PLAYER 1'S QUESTION: Roids is the slang name for which drug? Answer: Anabolic steroids.

PLAYER 2'S QUESTION: Weed is the nickname for which drug? Answer: Marijuana.

PLAYER 1'S QUESTION: What do the initials FAS stand for? Answer: Fetal alcohol syndrome.

PLAYER 2'S QUESTION: What does BAC stand for? Answer: Blood alcohol concentration.

PLAYER 1'S QUESTION: How do depressants enter the body? Answer: They are swallowed.

PLAYER 2'S QUESTION: What is the addictive stimulant found in tobacco? Answer: Nicotine.

PLAYER 1'S QUESTION: What group of drugs speeds up the mental process and puts the user on a high: stimulants, depressants, or hallucinogens? Answer: Stimulants.

Questions for Game 2

PLAYER 2'S QUESTION: Do filters on a cigarette eliminate the health risk for a smoker? Answer: No.

PLAYER 1'S QUESTION: Is alcohol high in calories? Answer: Yes.

PLAYER 2'S QUESTION: What is the term used to denote when two drugs combined produce a greater effect than if each drug were used alone? Answer: Synergism.

PLAYER 1'S QUESTION: What is the name of the process by which the liver burns up the consumed alcohol? Answer: Oxidation.

PLAYER 2'S QUESTION: What is the name of the liver disease caused by drinking heavily for a long period of time? Answer: Alcoholic Cirrhosis.

PLAYER 1'S QUESTION: What is the type of alcohol found in drinks? Answer: Ethyl.

PLAYER 2'S QUESTION: Which organ is responsible for oxidizing alcohol? Answer: The liver.

PLAYER 1'S QUESTION: What is the name of the black, sticky, cancer-causing substance in tobacco? Answer: Tar.

PLAYER 2'S QUESTION: Along with swallowing, injecting, and smoking, what is the fourth method of taking a drug? Answer: Sniffing.

Tic-Tac Drugs: Student Page

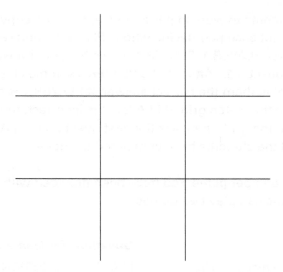

	Game 1	**Game 2**
ANSWER TO QUESTION 1	_____	_____
ANSWER TO QUESTION 2	_____	_____
ANSWER TO QUESTION 3	_____	_____
ANSWER TO QUESTION 4	_____	_____
ANSWER TO QUESTION 5	_____	_____
ANSWER TO QUESTION 6	_____	_____
ANSWER TO QUESTION 7	_____	_____
ANSWER TO QUESTION 8	_____	_____
ANSWER TO QUESTION 9	_____	_____

The Effects of Alcohol

Alcohol has both immediate and long-term side effects. Chronic alcohol use can cause many long-term problems. Below is a list of some of the effects of alcohol consumption. If the effect is short term, then write SHORT TERM in the space to the right. But if the effect is the result of long-term chronic use, then write LONG TERM in the space provided.

1. Slurs speech _____

2. Impairs reflexes and reaction times _____

3. Causes liver damage _____

4. Impairs judgment _____

5. Causes heart disease _____

6. Causes irreversible brain or nerve damage _____

7. Relaxes the eye muscles, making it difficult to focus _____

8. Reduces production of sex hormones _____

9. Increases frequency of urination _____

10. Causes cancer of the stomach _____

11. Causes nausea and vomiting _____

12. Causes malnutrition _____

13. May cause anger, violence, or mood swings _____

14. Causes diseases of the stomach, digestive system, pancreas _____

15. Results in a vitamin deficiency _____

Is Drinking a Problem for You?

Answer yes or no to the following questions by circling the appropriate response.

1. YES or NO: Do you sometimes drink alone?

2. YES or NO: Do your family or friends express concern about your drinking habits?

3. YES or NO: Do you occasionally have a drink when you first wake up?

4. YES or NO: Have you ever gone to school drunk?

5. YES or NO: Have you missed school because of a hangover or because you were too drunk to attend?

6. YES or NO: When you go out with friends, do you drink until you get drunk?

7. YES or NO: Do you drink to relax?

8. YES or NO: Do you lie about your drinking habits?

9. YES or NO: Do you ever pass out when you're drinking?

10. YES or NO: Do you get angry when others accuse you of having a drinking problem?

11. YES or NO: Do you guzzle drinks or drink shots in order to get drunk faster?

12. YES or NO: Do you do illegal or crazy things after drinking?

If you answered yes to any of these questions, you may want to rethink some of your drinking habits.

If you answered yes to six or more of these questions, then you may have a drinking problem and might want to seek counseling or help in order to deal with this issue.

Reasons, Reasons, Reasons

There are various reasons why teens drink alcohol. If you don't drink, think of people you know who do drink. If you have tried alcohol, think of the reasons why you tried it.

Instructions: Listed below are reasons why teens may try alcohol. Put a check mark in the box next to the reasons that apply to you or someone you know.

	- peer pressure or the need to fit in
	- rebellion
	- curiosity
	- to escape problems
	- encouraged or pressured by the media
	- for the "high" it gives you
	- to feel grown-up
	- to look cool
	- encouragement from parents or imitating parents
	- to relax
	- other (include your own reason) _____
	- other (include your own reason) _____

The Staircase of Decisions with Drinking

On the staircase shown below, place the letter representing each scenario on one of the steps. The top stair represents the most acceptable behavior and the bottom stair represents the least acceptable behavior.

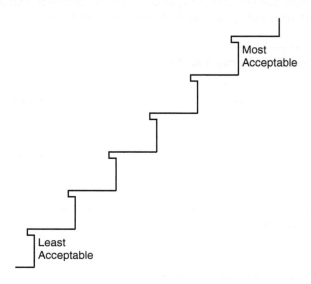

Most Acceptable

Least Acceptable

A. A teenage girl uses fake ID to get into a bar. While in the bar, she gets so drunk that she throws up in the washroom.

B. A 10-year-old boy takes a few sips of his dad's champagne during a New Year's party. His dad encouraged him to have the drink.

C. While baby-sitting, a 16-year-old boy opens the family's liquor cabinet and helps himself to a few shots of vodka before the parents come home. He does not tell the parents what he did.

D. A 17-year-old girl decides to drive her boyfriend home from a party because he is so drunk that he can't stand. The girl herself has had three drinks but feels fine enough to drive.

E. A group of teenagers skips a class and heads to a bar. They get drunk and head back to school for their class. In the class, they are noisy and disruptive.

F. Two kids sneak a bottle of vodka into a school dance. When some of the students aren't looking, the kids pour some of the vodka in the other students' soda.

NAME   DATE

The Gray of Alcoholism

Alcoholism is a difficult term to define. Some people consider themselves alcoholics and yet drink only once a week. Other alcoholics hide their drinking from family and friends, while still others drink openly with family and friends. Below are some descriptions of people and their drinking habits. Put a check mark in the alcoholic column if you consider this person to be an alcoholic. In the third column explain why you put the check mark there, or if you did not put a check mark, why you did not. On the back of this sheet, provide your definition of an alcoholic.

Scenario	Is this person an alcoholic or not?	Why or why not?
Micol teaches high school and likes to party. Because of the demands of his job, he only drinks on weekends. Micol usually drinks until he passes out on both Friday and Saturday nights throughout the year.		
Becca finds her job extremely stressful so she usually has a shot of vodka with her orange juice in the morning before she starts the day. She finds this helps her relax before work. She also believes that one shot is harmless, although she did recently try to stop her morning routine and found she could not.		
Quang is incredibly shy but works as a sales rep in an outgoing company. In his position, he often takes clients out for lunch or dinner. Whenever Quang does, he always has five or six drinks to relax. Clients agree that he's a funnier person when he's drunk.		
George has a glass of wine with dinner every night. His wife suggests that he try something different, but as a creature of habit, he refuses to give up his wine. His daily glass of wine is the only alcohol he ever drinks.		

What is your definition of the term *alcoholic*?

28

Thoughts About Drinking and Driving

Read the case below. First, respond as if you were the lawyer defending Anna, then as if you were the lawyer representing the parents of the victims.

> On the last day of school in June, the teachers of Bright High School hosted a party for all the twelfth-grade graduates. Although the teachers did not supply alcohol to this group of underage drinkers, many of the students sneaked alcohol into the party. One such student was Anna Kofski, who had five drinks.
>
> Anna's parents gave her the car that day so that she could drive some of her friends home from the party. Anna's parents had often told her never to drink and drive or to get into a car with a driver who had been drinking. They told her to call anytime she needed a ride in such a situation.
>
> Before leaving the party, Anna thought about calling her parents but decided against it because both her parents were working at the time and she did not want to be a nuisance. So Anna, despite the refusal of one of her friends to get into the car, drove home with two passengers.
>
> En route, she turned onto a street and drove on the wrong side of the road, causing the driver of a school bus to lose control of the bus while trying to avoid Anna's car. The bus flew down an embankment and the accident resulted in the death of all 25 passengers, who were young middle-school students, and the bus driver. Anna and her two passengers survived with no injuries.

1. On a separate piece of paper, explain how you would defend Anna if you were her lawyer. What arguments would you use to prevent her from being given a prison sentence or even the death penalty?

2. On another piece of paper, explain how you would argue the case if you were the lawyer for the families of the victims. What punishment do you think Anna deserves? What arguments would you use to try to have her convicted?

NAME _____   DATE _____

A Letter from a Child with FAS

Read the letter and answer the questions that follow on a separate piece of paper.

Dear pregnant mothers everywhere,

In a matter of months, you're going to be a new mom. You're probably getting ready for this upcoming day. I know that my mom painted the nursery walls blue and pink because she wasn't sure if I'd be a boy or a girl. She also went out with her friends regularly to celebrate the upcoming event and often had a few drinks, assuming that by drinking less than she had before she became pregnant, she wasn't causing me any harm.

She was wrong. I was born with FAS (fetal alcohol syndrome). When my mom drank, the alcohol quickly entered her bloodstream and then passed through the placenta to me in the womb. So when she had a drink, I had an equal amount of alcohol in my system. But because I was so much smaller than my mom, the alcohol had a much greater effect on me.

From the time I was a newborn, it was obvious I had FAS. I weighed less and was shorter than most other infants. Fortunately for me, I don't have the heart abnormalities or other physical defects that some FAS babies suffer from. However, like many children with FAS, I'm a behavioral problem at school and have such a short attention span that my teacher actually wrote this letter for me.

No one really knows how many children have FAS, although one study in Seattle estimates that one in every 900 pregnant moms delivers an FAS baby. Unfortunately, because there is no cure for FAS, this letter won't help me, but I hope it will help all the unborn babies of the future. If you're pregnant, please don't drink. It's amazing how little alcohol it takes to create someone like me. The good thing about this problem is that it can be prevented if you say no to that one glass of wine, bottle of beer, or evening cocktail.

Thanks for thinking of your baby.

Bobby White

1. What did you learn about FAS from this letter? What are some of the symptoms of FAS?

2. What is the cure for FAS?

3. Why did Bobby write this letter? Do you think he will succeed in his reason for writing this? Explain.

NAME _____ DATE _____

Express Yourself

Below are some controversial statements about drugs, alcohol, and smoking. Do you agree or disagree with each statement? Explain your opinions in the spaces provided and then share these opinions with your classmates.

1. Rock stars and other celebrities promote drug use.

   _____

   _____

   _____

2. All Olympic athletes should be tested for steroid use before and during the Olympics.

   _____

   _____

   _____

3. The legal drinking age should be lowered.

   _____

   _____

   _____

4. There should be a law against women smoking while pregnant.

   _____

   _____

   _____

5. Smoking cigarettes should be illegal.

   _____

   _____

   _____

NAME _____ DATE

Word Removal

Follow the instructions and cross out the appropriate words in the chart at the bottom of the page. Some words may be eliminated by more than one instruction. When you are finished, you will have a message that reads from left to right.

The message reads: _____

1. Cross out all three-letter words.

2. Cross out all the words in Columns 2, 3, and 4 that begin with the letter *s*.

3. Cross out all the words that rhyme with the word *three*.

4. Cross out all the words in Columns 1 and 4 that begin with the letter *a*.

5. Cross out all the contractions (for example, *can't*).

6. Cross out any words in Columns 2, 3, and 4 that start with letters from the last half of the alphabet.

7. Cross out any words in Column 1 that start with letters from the first half of the alphabet.

8. Cross out any words that consist of eight or more letters.

1	2	3	4
The	Park	Priority	Entertainment
Another	See	Should	Alcohol
Stay	Isn't	Won't	Fry
Blood	Ambulance	Bye	Relax
Let	Clean	Me	After
Don't	Tree	Influences	Legitimate
Just	Alcoholism	Avoid	Soap
A	Stoned	Tobacco	Be
All	Vitamin	Let's	Youth
Free	Wine	Problems	Drugs

SEX AND SEX-RELATED ISSUES

*Let a child start right in with the laws of Nature before
he's old enough to be surprised at them.*

Phyllis Bottome

Words and Slang

Slang words are often given to body parts and actions. For each word below, write all the slang words you can think of that mean the same thing. When you have compiled your list of slang words in each appropriate box, use another sheet of paper to answer the questions at the bottom of the page.

INTERCOURSE	BREASTS
PENIS	THUMB

1. Which word was the most difficult to find slang words for? Why do you think it was so difficult?

2. Which word has the most negative slang words? Why do you think this is the case?

3. Why do we use slang words for certain body parts? Who creates these slang words, and how do they become known to the rest of society?

Facts and Myths About Sex

People often confuse sexual facts with myths about sex. Determine whether each statement below is a fact or a myth. If the statement is true, circle the word FACT. If it is untrue, circle the word MYTH.

1. FACT or MYTH: All females are emotional during their period.

2. FACT or MYTH: A woman can get pregnant the first time she has sex.

3. FACT or MYTH: Women cannot swim and should not participate in physical activities during their period.

4. FACT or MYTH: A woman cannot become pregnant during her menstrual period.

5. FACT or MYTH: A woman cannot become pregnant if she is breast-feeding.

6. FACT or MYTH: If a woman showers after having sex, she won't get pregnant.

7. FACT or MYTH: Birth control pills and condoms may be ineffective if used after their expiration dates.

8. FACT or MYTH: Abstinence is the only form of birth control that is 100 percent effective.

9. FACT or MYTH: If a man ejaculates near the vagina, but not inside, he can still impregnate a woman.

10. FACT or MYTH: Young girls who have not yet started having their period cannot get pregnant.

11. FACT or MYTH: A boy may have one testicle that is larger than the other.

12. FACT or MYTH: When a boy has a wet dream, this is a signal that he is now producing sperm.

Reasons Why People Have Sex

There are many different reasons why people have sex. Some of these reasons are positive, some are negative, and some are either positive or negative depending on the person or situation. The following chart lists reasons why people have sex. For each reason, check the appropriate column. Do you view the reason as positive, negative, or both? At the end of the chart are two spaces where you can add two reasons people give for having sex that have not been mentioned.

People have sex...	Positive	Negative	Both
to have kids			
to control one's partner			
to make money			
to express love			
to exercise power			
to fulfill a need			
to satisfy one's sex drive			
to fulfill a fetish			
to harm			
to experience relaxation			
other_____			
other_____			

Sexuality Throughout Our Lifetime

Sexuality is one's total expression, thoughts, feelings, beliefs, and desires involving one's sexual being. Sexual needs and desires change during a lifetime. Complete the chart below by giving points of information about sexual awareness, sexual needs, and sexual desires at each stage of life. The first one (early childhood) is done for you as a guide.

Early Childhood (birth to age 4)	- experience pleasure by touching their genitals - explore body parts - begin to develop a male or female identity - mimic adults - like to cuddle, hug, and kiss
Late Childhood (ages 5-8)	
Pre-Adolescence (ages 9-13)	
Adolescence (ages 14-19)	
Early Adulthood (ages 20-30)	
Adulthood (ages 31-60)	
Late Adulthood (61 plus)	

The Four Phases of Sexual Intercourse

Below are descriptions of what occurs during each of the four phases of sexual intercourse. Place a 1 in the space next to the first phase of sexual intercourse, a 2 in the space next to the second phase, and so on.

_____ *The plateau phase:* This phase is an intense continuation of foreplay. During this phase the man's and the woman's heart rates and breathing rates increase, and blood pressures rise. The woman secretes fluid and her vagina lengthens and expands. The man's testicles increase in size and a tiny bit of fluid may come from the penis.

_____ *The resolution phase:* During this stage, both the man's and the woman's bodies, heart rates, breathing, and blood pressure return to a normal state.

_____ *The orgasmic phase:* This is the most intense moment of sex. During the male orgasm, the man ejaculates sperm. During the woman's orgasm, she too releases more fluid.

_____ *The excitement phase:* This is also sometimes called initial foreplay. In this phase, there is a transition from a normal state to a sexually aroused state. The man's penis becomes erect and the woman's vagina becomes moist. Both the man's and the woman's heart rates, breathing rates, and blood pressures begin to increase.

Male versus Female

Below is a list of female and male reproductive organs. If it is part of the female anatomy, check off the box in the female column; if it is part of the male anatomy, check off the box in the male column.

REPRODUCTIVE BODY PARTS	MALE	FEMALE
OVARIES		
TESTICLES		
PROSTATE GLAND		
FALLOPIAN TUBE		
SCROTUM		
CLITORIS		
PENIS		
SEMINAL VESICLE		
CERVIX		
EPIDIDYMIS		
UTERUS		
VAGINA		
COWPER'S GLANDS		
LABIA MINORA		
VAS DEFERENS		
LABIA MAJORA		
HYMEN		
ENDOMETRIUM		

The Birth Control Chart

A teacher was creating this birth control chart for his students but forgot to finish it. Help the teacher by providing the appropriate information in the chart where there are blank boxes.

Type	Effective-ness	How it is obtained	Advantages	Disadvantages
Abstinence		N/A		
Birth Control Pill			- the woman does not have to rely on the man for birth control - it is highly effective in preventing pregnancy	
The Latex Condom	85% higher if used with spermicide			- if it breaks or comes off during sex it is ineffective - if used incorrectly it is also ineffective - some people find it takes away some sexual pleasure
Hormone Implants or Injections		implanted in a woman's upper arm every 2 years or injected every 3 months by a physician		- does not prevent STIs (sexually transmitted infections) - the initial cost is very expensive - some women get irregular periods
Diaphragm			- the woman can determine the birth control	- does not prevent STIs (sexually transmitted infections) - can be awkward to insert and remove
IUD	97%		- very effective in preventing pregnancies - once it is inserted, a woman does not need to worry about it	

Birth Control Crossword

Across

4. This form of birth control is 100 percent effective.
6. This form of birth control can be described as having matchsticks in your arms.
9. This operation permanently sterilizes a woman (two words).
11. The act men and women engage in to have children.
15. Terminating a pregnancy.
17. What men ejaculate into women.
18. The number of months between conception and birth.
20. Emergency contraception called the M____ A ____ P____ by some (three words).
22. The short form for intrauterine device.

Down

1. This surgery permanently sterilizes a man.
2. This form of birth control is taken orally.
3. The place where a man inserts his penis into a woman.
5. Also called a rubber.
7. Giving the baby away.
8. Pulling the penis out of the vagina before ejaculation.
10. The result of conception and birth.
12. During an orgasm, a man _____ his sperm into a woman.
13. Another word for birth control.
14. A soft rubber cap place in the vagina that prevents sperm from entering the uterus.
16. Jellies, creams, and foams that contain chemicals to eliminate sperm.
19. What the man fertilizes in the woman.
21. The male body part that is inserted into the woman.

No Condom, No Sex: Talking to
Your Partner About Condoms

Imagine that you are about to have sex with your partner. Before foreplay begins, you produce a condom. Some people do not like using condoms even though they are very effective in preventing pregnancy and STIs (sexually transmitted infections). Below are some excuses your partner may give for why he or she does not want to use a condom. For each excuse, provide a response that clearly informs your partner why that excuse isn't acceptable.

Excuse: "We've never used a condom before. Why do we need to start now?"

Your response: _____

_____

Excuse: "I don't like using condoms because they take away from the pleasure."

Your response: _____

_____

Excuse: "Using a condom makes me feel like you don't trust me. I don't have any diseases, trust me."

Your response: _____

_____

Excuse: "Using a condom isn't romantic. It ruins the mood when we have to stop to put it on."

Your response: _____

_____

Excuse: "If you want to use a condom, then I don't want to have sex."

Your response: _____

_____

Dr. Birth Control

Imagine that you are a doctor. The following paragraphs present information about some of your patients who have come to ask your advice on birth control. For each patient, prescribe a form of birth control and explain why you picked that particular form. Forms of birth control you may wish to consider include these:

condoms	vaginal sponge	hormonal injections
IUD	tubal ligation	birth control pill
abstinence	vasectomy	diaphragm
	progestin implants (for example, Norplant™)	

1. Fatima is 13 years old and her boyfriend Shahzad is 16. Shahzad wants to have sex with her. Fatima is a virgin, but Shahzad is not. Fatima admits that she doesn't really want to have sex and isn't sure she's ready. In fact, she wants to use birth control that's 100 percent effective because she's definitely not ready to have a baby.

Form of birth control that you recommend: _____

Reasons: _____

2. Rory and his wife Cory have been married for one year. They are not worried about sexually transmitted infections, but they are not ready to have children.

Form of birth control that you recommend: _____

Reasons: _____

3. Kesha and her boyfriend Eduardo, both age 20, have been dating for three months. They have both been sexually active in previous relationships although they now agree to be monogamous. In spite of this, Kesha is worried that Eduardo may have an STI from a previous relationship.

Form of birth control that you recommend: _____

Reasons: _____

4. Tara and Barry just got married. Before marriage, they dated for six years and know that they are disease-free. They have both decided they don't want to have children for at least five years.

Form of birth control that you recommend: _____

Reasons: _____

NAME   DATE

Some Thoughts on Abstinence

Instructions: Read this article and use the information in the article to complete the chart that follows.

Although some people think "everybody's doing it," many teens believe that abstinence is a better option than having sex. Naneesh Brown, for example, wants her wedding night to be the most special night of her life. This means that she doesn't want to have sex until that night. She believes that her true love will understand and respect her desires.

Naneesh's friend, Mohammed, also plans to wait until marriage before having sex, but his reason is different. Mohammed's mom got pregnant when she was in her teens and gave birth to Mohammed and his twin brother. Mohammed wants to wait because he doesn't want to repeat his mom's early entrance into parent-hood. Although Mohammed feels his mom did a great job raising him and his brother, he also thinks she sacrificed her own dreams when becoming a parent. Mohammed figures by not having sex, he won't have to worry at all about getting a girl pregnant.

Tina and John have also chosen abstinence. They were once sexually active, but they found that sex ruined a perfectly good relationship. Once they started having sex, their relationship became so obsessed with when and where they'd have sex that they stopped having fun together and were fighting all the time. They decided to stop having sex until they got older and could maintain a sexual relationship without losing the spark.

Raneem doesn't want to have sex yet because, at age 16, she thinks having sex too early will ruin her reputation. Raneem believes that once she has sex with one boyfriend it will be too easy to have sex with the next guy she dates, and she doesn't want to be dating in her twenties only to find that she's slept with a dozen guys.

Finally, Cassie is waiting to have sex because of religious reasons. She doesn't want to let her church and herself down by having sex out of wedlock.

All of these people have different reasons but the end result is the same: they've chosen abstinence and they're not ashamed to admit it.

The Some-Thoughts-on-Abstinence Chart

NAME	REASONS FOR CHOOSING ABSTINENCE	YOUR THOUGHTS CONCERNING THIS REASON
Naneesh		
Mohammed		
Tina and John		
Raneem		
Cassie		

What Should Vanessa Do?

Vanessa is a twelfth-grade honors student who hopes to attend college in the fall on a full academic scholarship. She started dating Dan, a football player, three months ago. Although Vanessa was a virgin and planned to stay that way for a few more years, Dan persuaded her one night after a party to have sex with him. Even though Vanessa was fairly drunk, she was coherent enough to agree to sex and insist that Dan wear a condom. Unfortunately, the condom broke while they had sex and Vanessa became pregnant. When Vanessa discovered she was pregnant, she turned to four people for advice.

Instructions: Read the advice of the four people. In the chart that follows each person's advice, indicate the pros and cons of each suggestion Vanessa is offered.

1. When Dan finds out, he proposes to Vanessa and suggests they get married, quit school, get jobs, and raise the baby.

Pros	Cons

2. When Vanessa's mom finds out, she insists that Vanessa keep the baby, live at home, and attend college part-time in the fall. This college, unfortunately, is not the one that has offered Vanessa a scholarship, and it does not offer any of the programs she wants to take.

Pros	Cons

3. When Vanessa's dad finds out, he believes the right solution is for Vanessa to give the baby up for adoption.

Pros	Cons

4. When Vanessa's best friend Maggie finds out, she suggests that Vanessa get an abortion.

Pros	Cons

NAME _____   DATE _____

Facts About Adoption

Decide whether or not each fact about adoption is true or false. (The source for the information in this quiz is the National Council for Adoption.)

1. TRUE or FALSE: Two out of three American children who are waiting to be adopted have some type of special need.

2. TRUE or FALSE: It is easier to find an adoptive family for visibly minority children than for white children.

3. TRUE or FALSE: More than half the children who are waiting to be adopted in the United States have been waiting for two years or more.

4. TRUE or FALSE: Between 50 and 70 percent of the children who are placed in foster care eventually return to their parents.

5. TRUE or FALSE: A few years ago almost half of the adoptions were of healthy infants of all races and ethnic backgrounds.

6. TRUE or FALSE: Most adopted children search for their birth parents when they become adults.

7. TRUE or FALSE: Studies have proven that adopted children enjoy more socioeconomic benefits than children who remain with their unmarried birth mother.

8. TRUE or FALSE: It is more difficult for a child with special needs to find an adoptive home than for a healthy child.

9. TRUE or FALSE: The median age of U.S. children waiting to be adopted is 7.8 years of age.

10. TRUE or FALSE: Between 5 and 10 million couples in the United States want to adopt children.

NAME _____ DATE _____

What to Avoid During Pregnancy

When women are pregnant, they need to be very conscious of the foods they eat and what they drink and the activities they engage in because some food, drink, and activities may harm the child they are carrying. The following is a list of actions. If the action mentioned is something a pregnant woman should avoid, put a check mark in the avoid column. If the activity is something that would be good for a pregnant woman, put a check mark in the OKAY column.

ACTIVITY	AVOID	OKAY
1. drinking alcohol		
2. drinking milk		
3. dyeing your hair		
4. cleaning the cat's litter box		
5. drinking water		
6. eating fruits and vegetables		
7. smoking cigarettes		
8. sitting in a sauna, steam room, or hot tub		
9. handling or eating uncooked meat		
10. taking folic acid (vitamin B) daily		
11. taking illegal, prescription, or over-the-counter drugs		
12. having an X ray		
13. drinking coffee		
14. going for walks		

Stages in the Womb

Each item listed below describes a stage in the development of a baby in the womb. For each stage, determine whether this occurs during the first month, second month, third month, fourth month, sixth month, or ninth month of development.

1. By the end of the _____ month:
   The baby grows to eight inches tall and is strong enough that small movements may
     be felt by the mother.
   The baby's own placenta becomes fully established.
   The amount of amniotic fluids that the baby is floating in increases dramatically.

2. By the end of the _____ month:
   The embryo has all its organs in miniature.
   Fingers and toes begin to emerge.
   The mouth has lips and a tongue begins to form.
   The embryo is called a fetus.

3. By the end of the _____ month:
   The heart begins to beat.
   The baby is one-quarter inch long.
   At the beginning of this month, the fertilized egg makes its way down the fallopian
     tubes to the uterus.
   The baby is called an embryo.

4. By the end of the _____ month:
   The baby's hearing is excellent and she can recognize her mother's voice.
   Because the baby is growing and needs extra space, there is less amniotic fluid.
   There is now a difference between sleeping and waking.
   The baby puts on the bulk of his weight.

5. By the end of the _____ month:
   The baby's movements can be felt by people who touch the mother's belly.
   The baby can suck her thumb.
   The baby begins to show auditory response to sound, although the hearing
     apparatus is not fully mature.
   By the end of this period, the eyelids become unsealed and the baby can open his eyes.

6. By the end of the _____ month:
   The eyelids grow large enough to cover the eyes.
   The baby can roll over from front to back but she is still too small for the mother to
     feel this.
   The baby does not sleep yet but moves constantly.
   The diaphragm begins to work.

STI (STD) Unscramble

Unscramble each of the following words to determine the name of the STI (sexually transmitted infection).

1. IDAS

2. NTLAIEG PEERHS

3. YHISISPL

4. HONAEROGR

5. DHYCALAIM

6. TNEALGI SRTAW

7. BCUPI CELI

8. PTTAIISEH B

Dr. STI (STD)

Unfortunately, many Americans have been infected with STIs (sexually transmitted infections). Below are three scenarios. For each scenario decide which type of STI the person has been infected with and what treatment (if any) is available.

1. Darv has lost a lot of weight lately. At night he sweats more than usual. He's tired all the time and has noticed purple blotches on his skin.

What STI has Darv been infected with? _____

What treatment is available? _____

_____

2. Bobby-Sue had unprotected sex a week ago and now has a cluster of blisters inside her vagina that are not painful. (In fact, she does not even realize they are there.) She also has flu-like symptoms, a fever, and headaches.

What STI has Bobby-Sue been infected with? _____

What treatment is available? _____

_____

3. Carl's pubic hair is itchy all the time, especially at night, and he can see bugs moving through the hair.

What STI has Carl been infected with? _____

What treatment is available? _____

_____

Ways of Acquiring HIV

HIV is a serious disease that affects millions of people around the world. Although people fear getting the disease, there are ways to protect yourself from acquiring HIV. The following chart lists methods for acquiring HIV. If the method is a false one, put an X in the NO column, but if the method is an actual way of acquiring HIV, put an X in the YES column.

WAYS OF ACQUIRING HIV	NO	YES
1. Through a mosquito bite or another insect bite		
2. Having unprotected sexual intercourse with someone infected with HIV		
3. Sitting on a toilet seat where an HIV victim sat		
4. Hugging someone infected with HIV		
5. Sharing a syringe or needle with someone infected with HIV		
6. Having someone who has HIV sneeze or cough near you		
7. Becoming artificially inseminated with the sperm of a man infected with HIV		
8. Donating blood		
9. Using the comb or brush of someone infected with HIV		
10. Sharing eating utensils with someone infected with HIV		
11. Receiving a transfusion of blood infected with HIV		
12. Receiving an organ from a donor infected with HIV		
13. Shaking the hands of someone infected with HIV		
14. A mother with HIV breastfeeding an infant may have infected the infant		

Attitudes About AIDS: We've Come a Long Way Since the 1980s

In the 1980s, AIDS was a new disease that people knew very little about. As a result, people jumped to conclusions and there were many misconceptions about this disease. Listed below are a few of the types of comments people used to make about AIDS. In the space provided, explain what is untrue or incorrect about each comment.

On one talk show in 1987, a man explained that he thought all AIDS patients should live in isolation for the safety of the rest of society.

_____

_____

_____

Many people worried that if they swam in a swimming pool where an AIDS-infected person had swum, they might get the AIDS virus. People expressed the same thought about toilets. They thought AIDS could spread from toilet seats.

_____

_____

_____

In the space below, explain how misinformation about AIDS can hurt AIDS patients. What can you do to make sure that people learn the right facts about AIDS and how it is spread?

_____

_____

_____

_____

_____

_____

NAME   DATE

A Poem About an AIDS Victim

Read the poem and answer the questions that follow on a separate piece of paper.

Mr. Pinnington

Everyone in the town of Saltaire
(Which had a population of 1,172
Even though the sign at the entrance
To the town stated "Population: 1,000")
Knew that Mr. Pinnington,
The local piano teacher,
Was homosexual.

Mr. Pinnington never publicly
Acknowledged this,
But somehow
Everyone in the town
Just knew.

Then the town was in a state of shock
When the doctor's wife
Told the librarian,
Who told my Sunday school teacher,
Who told my mother
(In the strictest of confidence)
That Mr. Pinnington had AIDS.

He told all his piano students
(And the rest of the town)
That he had cancer.
He stopped teaching piano;
He stopped playing the piano;
And eventually he died
Alone.

What saddened me most after his death
Was that we all knew his diagnosis
And no one told him
That we all knew
And not to be afraid to live the truth.

S. McTavish

1. What was Mr. Pinnington's reaction to acquiring AIDS?

2. Why do you think he reacted this way?

3. What is the narrator's reaction to Mr. Pinnington's disease and what is meant by the line "And not to be afraid to live the truth"?

4. Why should society accept and help AIDS patients?

Facts About Homosexuality

Here are some facts about homosexuality. Are they true or false? Circle the correct response to each one.

1. TRUE or FALSE: All people who are gay choose to be gay.

2. TRUE or FALSE: In the United States, approximately 10 percent of women are lesbians and 10 percent of men are homosexual.

3. TRUE or FALSE: Homosexuals do not like being in committed, monogamous relationships.

4. TRUE or FALSE: You can tell if someone is gay by looking at him or her. Lesbians look and dress like men, and homosexual men look and act effeminate.

5. TRUE or FALSE: The suicide rate among homosexuals is three times the rate among heterosexuals.

6. TRUE or FALSE: A gay person who is not sexually active is not gay.

7. TRUE or FALSE: About 95 percent of all sexual abuse toward children is committed by homosexuals.

8. TRUE or FALSE: In all 50 states, it is legal for homosexuals to marry.

Options for Couples Who Want a Child
(But Are Having Infertility Problems)

When an infertile couple is having trouble conceiving a child, they have various options to help them become parents. Some of these options involve reproductive technologies that help them conceive a child. Four options are listed below. Try to come up with a definition for each option based on your own knowledge, class discussion, or Internet search.

Artificial insemination: _____

_____

_____

Artificial insemination by a donor: _____

_____

_____

In vitro fertilization/embryo transfer: _____

_____

_____

In vitro fertilization with an egg donor: _____

_____

_____

Surrogate Rights

One option for an infertile couple who want to have a child is to use a surrogate mother. The term *surrogate* means a person who acts as, or takes the place of, another person.

The rights of surrogate parents vary from state to state. Some states allow surrogate parents visitation rights, while others do not. Since the rights vary, there is a lot of controversy over the rights of surrogate parents. Read the following scenario and decide what rights you think this particular surrogate mother should have. Write your opinion in the space provided. (Continue on the back of this sheet, if necessary.)

> Martin and his wife, Juanita, had the embryo that came from Martin's sperm and Juanita's egg implanted in a surrogate mother. After the baby is born, the surrogate mother asks for visiting rights to see the baby monthly. Martin and Juanita do not want this; in fact, before the birth they had the woman sign an agreement to say that she would not visit the child. However, the surrogate mother now says that everything changed when she gave birth, and that she could not predict how she would feel before the baby was born. The surrogate mother has three children of her own and would like to have more, but her husband is against it.

Do you think the surrogate mother should have any rights to see the baby? Explain.

_____

_____

_____

_____

_____

_____

_____

_____

NAME _____   DATE _____

Sexual Harassment Facts

What is sexual harassment? According to the *Gage Canadian Dictionary,* sexual harassment is "unwelcome sexual advances, sexual comments, etc., directed toward someone by a fellow employee, an employer, or a superior, especially if compliance constitutes a form of blackmail" (1998, p. 1340).

Decide if each of the following statements about sexual harassment is true or false. If the statement is false, explain in the space provided what changes need to be made to make the statement true.

1. TRUE or FALSE: Sexual harassment only happens to women.

   _____

   _____

2. TRUE or FALSE: Women who dress provocatively deserve to be sexually harassed.

   _____

   _____

3. TRUE or FALSE: If a person makes lewd sexual comments, this is never sexual harassment.

   _____

   _____

4. TRUE or FALSE: Almost 50 percent of American female college students experience some form of sexual harassment.

   _____

   _____

5. TRUE or FALSE: If you are being sexually harassed, there is nothing you can do to stop it.

   _____

   _____

Many people say that sexual harassment is about power and not sex. On the back of this sheet, explain why many people think some use sexual harassment to obtain power.

Sexual Harassment or Not Sexual Harassment?

For each scenario or comment determine if this is or is not an example of sexual harassment. Then explain your decision in the space provided.

1. A boss says to an employee, "If you sleep with me, I'll make sure you get that promotion."

Is this or is this not an example of sexual harassment?

Comment: _____

2. A guy says to his girlfriend, "You look so sexy in that dress that I want to have sex with you."

Is this or is this not an example of sexual harassment?

Comment: _____

3. A professor jokes to his students, "I'm not sure why so many women are taking this class. Your place is at home in the kitchen."

Is this or is this not an example of sexual harassment?

Comment: _____

4. A male teacher invites a female student to meet him late at night at his place to study for an exam. He tells her that he wants to get to know her better. She shows up and he's got candles and soft music playing and doesn't seem to want to study.

Is this or is this not an example of sexual harassment?

Comment: _____

5. A boss pats his secretary on the rear as she passes by his desk.

Is this or is this not an example of sexual harassment?

Comment: _____

6. A woman congratulates her male employees who win the employee-of-the-month award with a kiss on the lips. She always threatens that if they don't kiss her, she'll take their award away.

Is this or is this not an example of sexual harassment?

Comment: _____

Date Rape

Date rape has become a serious problem in America. According to statistics, one in four female college students reports having been raped, or had a rape attempted, before they graduated.

What is date rape? In the space provided, come up with a definition for date rape.

_____

_____

_____

According to Patricia Martens Miller in her book *Sex Is Not a Four-Letter Word!* (1994), the type of man who rapes can be described as follows:

- Is extremely jealous
- Likes to dominate and control all situations
- Enjoys humiliating and manipulating women
- Drinks excessively
- Believes his sexual urges are uncontrollable
- Is aggressive

What can women do when on a date to avoid date rape? In the space provided, suggest five things women can do to try to prevent it.

1. _____

2. _____

3. _____

4. _____

5. _____

Date-Rape Decisions

For each situation below, decide if the people have done anything wrong and if they should or should not be punished. If you think they should be punished, what form should the punishment take? Write your comments on the back of this sheet.

Situation I

Carol studied all night and then overslept through the time her exam was given. Carol is a straight-A student, but if she does not pass this exam, she will fail the course and ruin her academic record. Carol is hoping to get an academic scholarship to college, so she can't afford to fail the course. Carol's teacher is tough, and Carol knows if she tells him the truth, he'll fail her. So she makes up a story about being abducted by a guy in a red pickup truck and raped. After hearing Carol's story, the teacher calls the police. By noon, they have three suspects who own red pickup trucks in for questioning. Did Carol do something wrong? Should she be punished? Explain.

Situation II

Celeste and Jacob have been dating for six months. They are both virgins, but they have decided to have sex. On the night they plan to do so, Celeste is very keen. She wears a sexy outfit and bathes herself in perfume. Jacob has lit candles everywhere and has romantic music playing. The two quietly speed through foreplay and Jacob enters Celeste. As soon as this happens, Celeste decides she no longer wants to have sex and tells him to stop. Jacob says he can't stop and continues to have sex until he comes. Afterward, Celeste accuses Jacob of raping her. Did Jacob do something wrong? Should he be punished? Explain.

Situation III

Guy invites Linda on a date. The two have been friends since sixth grade but have never been on a date together before. Guy takes Linda out for dinner, and the two share a bottle of wine. Afterward, they go back to Guy's place where he gives Linda more drinks. Guy starts kissing Linda. She forcefully tells him that she does not like getting physical on the first date. He accuses her of playing hard to get and continues to fondle her. She begs him to stop. Rather than stop, Guy rips off Linda's clothes, pins her to the couch, and has sex with her. Has Guy done anything wrong? Should he be punished? Explain.

Finish the Story

Read the following story and then write how you think the story would end based on the two optional endings.

Giao and his girlfriend, Lesley, started dating two years ago after meeting at a school dance. Now in twelfth grade, the two have never had sex because Lesley wants to wait until she gets married. Lately, Giao's friends have been teasing him because he hasn't had sex yet. He feels like he's the only guy who is a virgin. Although he used to respect Lesley's views on premarital sex, he's started pressuring her to have sex.

The pressure got to Lesley so much that two weeks ago she broke up with Giao. The breakup devastated both of them because they really loved each other a lot. Giao feels awful for pressuring Lesley, and he's asked her to come to his place to talk things over. Lesley has also regretted the breakup and is torn between sticking to her values and satisfying Giao's needs. She is excited about meeting him at his place and dresses in an outfit that turns him on. After an hour of discussing things and admitting they both miss each other, the two begin to kiss. Then Giao announces that his parents won't be home for hours and pulls out a condom.

1. Write a plausible ending in which Lesley refuses to have sex.

   _____

   _____

   _____

2. Write a plausible ending in which Lesley agrees to have sex.

   _____

   _____

   _____

3. How do your endings compare with those of your classmates?

   _____

   _____

   _____

Dear Rudy . . .

Here are some letters for Rudy the Relationship Counselor. Rudy, however, is on holiday, so you have been asked to write the responses. Write your responses on a separate piece of paper.

Dear Rudy,

My boyfriend and I have been together for two years. We love each other very much and know that we want to get married. The only problem is that we need our parents' consent because we are only 16 years old. Both our parents say that we are too young to get married, but we disagree. What do you think we should do? Are we too young to get married?

From Sally in Silverdale

Dear Rudy,

I just found out that my girlfriend Nancy has cheated on me with my best friend, Rob. Nancy and I haven't been together for long, but Rob knows how much I care for her. I found out that they cheated because Nancy's sister's boyfriend told me they were caught making out at a party last week. I want to be with Nancy but not if she wants to be with Rob. What should I do?

From Cheated-on-Charlie in Chilliwack

Dear Rudy,

My boyfriend, Leroy, is 19, and I'm 17. We've been together for a year and a half. He thinks it's time we slept together. I'm not sure whether or not I'm ready. Leroy said he'd wait until I'm ready, but he's putting a lot of pressure on me to say yes. He says he can't wait much longer. I'm worried that he might look elsewhere if I don't do it, but I also know that I'm not ready. What should I do?

From Jackie in Jarvis

NAME   DATE

Sex Jeopardy

This game is similar to the TV game show *Jeopardy.* As in *Jeopardy,* answer as many questions as you can by writing the answer in the box under the question. Unlike *Jeopardy,* you do not need to phrase it in the form of a question. When you are done, calculate your score. The questions in the top row are worth 100 points each, the questions in the second row are worth 200 points each, and so on.

	Saying No to Pregnancy	The ABCs of STIs	She Parts	He Parts	Talk the Talk (Sex Vocab.)
100	What form of birth control is taken orally 21 or 28 days a month?	Which STI can you obtain from unprotected sex, a shared needle, or a blood transfusion?	What does a sperm fertilize to create a baby?	What fertilizes a woman's egg to create a baby?	Which gender gets a pap smear?
200	What is most effective in preventing pregnancy and HIV infection?	Which STI makes you itchy because of the insect bites?	When a woman has sex, the man's penis enters what?	During sex what erect male body part enters the female?	What does STI stand for?
300	What birth control is 100% effective because it avoids intimate contacts?	What STI has tiny cauliflower-like warts on your genitals?	Where are woman's eggs produced?	Where are sperm produced?	What is the male hormone that causes puberty?
400	What form of birth control needs to be inserted into the woman before having sex?	There is no cure for which STI? It is not AIDS or HIV but does begin with the letter H and has 6 letters.	During ovulation, a mature egg enters one of two —what?	What is the tube called that carries urine and semen from the body?	When an unfertilized egg leaves the body, this process is called—what?
500	What form of birth control does the doctor insert into the woman and remove?	Which STI can sometimes be undetected and begins with the letter C?	When a woman's egg is fertilized by the male, where does it go?	Each testicle is protected by a sac called —what?	What is it called when men have an uncontrolled ejaculation during sleep?

62

It Takes Three

Use the following words to fill in the blank spaces on the chart below. Each word may be used only once, and each space must take a word that fits the description in the left-hand column.

fallopian tube	gonorrhea	testosterone	placenta	premature ejaculation
birth control pill	epididymis	genital warts	AIDS	progesterone
penis	fetus	estrogen	sponge	diaphragm
impotence	vaginal	embryo	anal	vaginismus
condom	ovary	chlamydia	uterus	genital herpes
oral	Norplant™	scrotum	syphilis	spermicide

Parts of the female sexual anatomy			
Parts of the male sexual anatomy			
Birth control that is used only during sex			
Male and female hormones			
Stages of development in the womb			
Chemical birth control			
Methods of sex that can spread HIV			
Sexual problems			
STIs (sexually transmitted infections) that begin with the letter G			
STIs (sexually transmitted infections)			

NAME   DATE

Alphabet Soup

There are 26 empty boxes in the middle of the chart below. Insert a different letter of the alphabet into each box to form a word of five or more letters when you read across. The letter you add may be from the beginning, middle, or end of the word. All the letters in the row may not necessarily be part of the word. All the words are related to sex and sexual issues.

V	W	U	D	I		E	N	I	S	R
P	E	N	O	V		I	S	S	E	S
W	O	M	I	H		M	E	N	O	R
F	E	T	V	A		I	N	A	U	S
O	P	R	E	G		A	N	T	A	C
P	I	L	M	A		O	N	D	O	M
K	W	I	T	H		R	A	W	A	L
O	V	D	T	E		T	E	S	T	E
J	A	M	T	C		A	R	T	S	L
M	E	N	C	E		V	I	X	Y	Z
L	O	V	E	I		E	T	U	S	S
I	U	T	E	R		S	W	O	M	D
B	L	M	N	L		B	I	A	O	P
C	A	N	Y	O		Y	G	O	T	E
A	V	W	S	E		U	A	L	T	M
S	S	P	E	R		E	I	V	H	T
C	O	N	S	E		U	E	N	C	E
R	S	C	R	O		U	M	D	F	H
B	O	X	E	L		E	L	L	Y	Z
S	F	E	R	T		L	E	V	I	R
K	J	S	E	M		R	Y	O	D	G
B	C	L	I	T		R	I	S	M	S
E	N	O	R	P		A	N	T	W	E
E	D	I	A	P		R	A	G	M	T
F	I	X	O	O		U	L	A	T	E
G	P	L	A	C		N	T	A	H	I

LOVE, RELATIONSHIPS, MARRIAGE, AND FAMILY

*Seven years would be insufficient to make some people
acquainted with each other, and seven days are
more than enough for others.*

Jane Austen

NAME _____   DATE _____

A Relationship Balloon Tree

A well-known proverb states, "No one is an island." This is very true. In life, we have many relationships and friendships with people who have a positive or negative influence on us. Fill in the balloons on the balloon tree with the names of family, friends, and others who have had a positive influence on you over the years and provided you with love, friendship, or lessons about life. You will use these names in the next exercise.

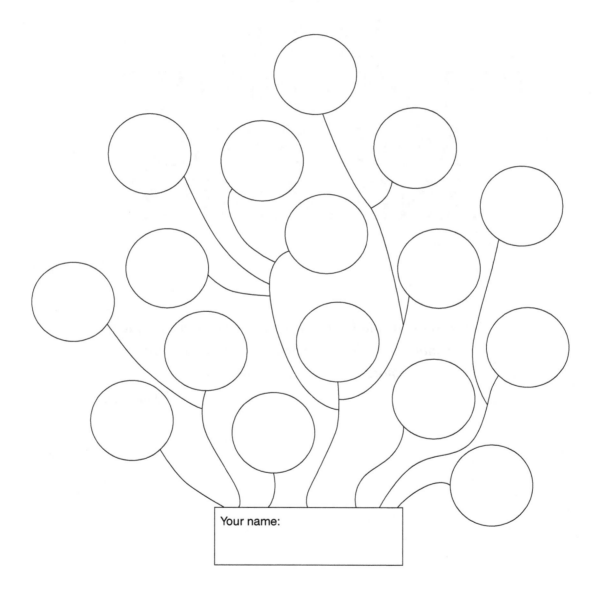

The Relationship Chart

Choose five names from the previous Relationship Balloon Tree and put them in the name column. Then complete the chart for each of these five people. The chart will help you examine the significance of these people in your life.

Name	Their relationship to you (i.e., friend, teacher, parent, etc.)	How long have you known this person?	In point form, explain what makes this person a positive influence in your life.
Person 1			
Person 2			
Person 3			
Person 4			
Person 5			

NAME _____ DATE _____

Circle of Friends

We all have friends, but some are closer than others. This exercise will allow you to reflect on the different degrees of closeness you have with your friends.

Many people have one or two best friends. These people are the ones you confide in the most. In the center circle, write the name(s) of your best friend(s).

Next, you usually have a group of close friends (your best friend is often in this group) whom you see regularly. These people also know a lot about you, and you probably find it easy to open up to this group. Write the names of your close friends in the middle circle.

Finally, we have many acquaintances in life. These are people with whom we enjoy spending time, but we may not open up to them and reveal inner thoughts or feelings. We also don't usually spend as much time with our acquaintances as we do with our close friends. In the outside circle, write the names of some of your acquaintances.

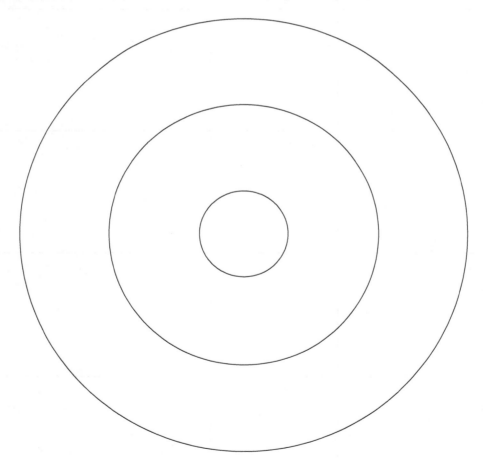

NAME _____   DATE

Different Friends, Different Occasions

During your lifetime, you will have a number of different friends. Some friendships will last longer than others. You will also discover that different friends meet different needs. For instance, you may be interested in watching movies with one friend but playing sports with another.

Write the name in the space provided of the friend most likely to accompany you in the following situations. (Try to use a different person for each situation.)

Which friend would you call if . . .

1. You were going to watch a professional sport live? _____

2. You were going to an art gallery? _____

3. You needed help with your homework in your worst subject? _____

4. You needed to tell someone a secret? _____

5. You had to shop for clothes? _____

6. You were going to see a stand-up comic perform? _____

7. You needed a shoulder to cry on? _____

8. You were going to a concert to hear your favorite band or musician?

   _____

9. You were going to the library to pick out a book for pleasure reading?

   _____

10. You were going on a bike ride or out for a jog? _____

NAME _____   DATE

All About Cliques

In your lifetime, you will meet many different types of friends, and you will probably form friendships with a close group of friends. It is natural for a group of friends to hang out together, but a group can be negative if it becomes a clique. A clique is usually a group of people who form negative judgments of others and will not allow others to enter their circle of friends. Below is a list of actions taken by groups of friends. If the action would likely be taken by a positive group of friends, put an X in the positive group column. If the action is the negative action of a clique, put an X in the clique column.

	CLIQUE	POSITIVE
1. The people in the group all dress the same and tease each other if they don't dress identically.		
2. The group goes out of its way to make a new person feel welcome.		
3. The people in the group spend all their time doing things together and alienate anyone who does his/her own thing or has another group of friends.		
4. The group only associates with people who have the same interests or personality.		
5. At a social activity (like a school dance), members of the group mingle with other groups of friends.		
6. The group of friends is friendly with everyone, even if these people are considered unpopular.		
7. The group gossips about other people who are outside its own circle and makes fun of them behind their backs.		

Try to think of at least three ways that a clique can become a more positive group.

1. _____

_____

2. _____

_____

3. _____

_____

NAME _____   DATE _____

Break the Clique

Each of the following scenarios describes a clique of friends acting insensitively toward someone else. In the space provided, describe how, if you were a member of the group, you would make the situation more positive for the new person.

Scenario 1

You play on the basketball team. All the members on the team have played together for at least three years. This year an amazing player transfers from another team and quickly demonstrates that he or she is much better than the former superstar of your team. The superstar of your team immediately dislikes this player and makes every attempt possible to put him or her down. Many of your teammates follow the superstar's example; they avoid passing the ball to the new player or talking to him or her in the locker room.

What can you do to make things more positive for this new player?

_____

_____

_____

_____

_____

Scenario 2

A new student has joined your class. Your teacher announces that his family has moved here to escape the war-torn country they are from. He doesn't speak much English and it is obvious that his family is quite poor because he wears the same clothes every day. By the end of the first week, all of your friends have decided they dislike this new boy and they either make fun of him or ignore him completely.

What can you do to make things more positive for this new student?

_____

_____

_____

_____

Finish the Sentences on Dating

Here are a number of incomplete sentences. Finish each sentence with your own thoughts on dating.

1. On a first date, I think it is appropriate to _____

   _____

2. On a first date, I think it is inappropriate to _____

   _____

3. The appropriate age to start dating is _____

   _____

4. My parents would disapprove if I dated someone who _____

   _____

5. If a guy or girl whom I ask on a date turns me down, I feel _____

   _____

6. The ideal date would consist of _____

   _____

7. If the person I was dating did something that I didn't like, I would _____

   _____

8. The most important quality my date should have is _____

   _____

9. A quality that I would not tolerate in a person I date is _____

   _____

10. As far as dating in a group, I am _____

    _____

The Singles Ads

Many people today find it difficult to meet that special person, so they sometimes use singles ads in the newspapers as a means of meeting someone who might share similar interests. Read the ads below and decide which one appeals to you the most. Why does it appeal? At the bottom of the page, write your own singles ad.

1. In search of a lifemate who likes taking long walks, going to films and plays, and curling up on the couch on a rainy day and watching movies. This person must also value family and be career-oriented. If you're the one, respond to this ad by calling 825-6776.

2. Sports. Sports. Sports. I love sports and I want to date someone who loves them too. If you love playing sports, watching sports, and dreaming sports, then call me today at 234-5678.

3. Whoever said that "looks don't matter" is crazy. I want someone who is really attractive. You don't need to share my interests or have any of your own—just look good. If you're this person, send me a photo at 123 Road St., City, ST 12345.

4. True friends are hard to find and a lifemate is even harder. I'm searching for a friend who enjoys music, movies, and going out and doing things. And hopefully, this friendship may slowly evolve into a relationship, which might just evolve into marriage. If you're interested in being this type of friend, call me at 123-4567.

5. I want to see the world and am looking for someone who also loves to travel. I also want to go on adventures like snowboarding in Canada, bungy jumping in Australia, and mountain climbing in Switzerland. If you want to join me on some adventures, call me at 765-4321.

Which ad appeals to you the most? Why? _____

_____

Which ad appeals to you the least? Why? _____

_____

Create a singles ad for yourself. _____

_____

_____

_____

_____

NAME _____   DATE

How Do Couples Meet?

In the left-hand column of the chart below is a list of different ways that couples meet. In the spaces indicated, write down one or two advantages and disadvantages of each way of meeting.

Ways Couples Meet	Advantages	Disadvantages
Through friends or family		
At work or at college		
Through a dating service or singles ads		
At a bar or at a party		
Through e-mail or a chatroom		
Through a sports team, music group, church group, or another extracurricular activity		

NAME_____   DATE

Steps in a Relationship

Just as people are unique, so too are their attitudes in relationships. For example, one person might feel more comfortable making out than saying "I love you," while another person might say "I love you" weeks before being ready to make out.

Think of how you act, or might act, in a significant romantic relationship. Look at the following list of actions. Put a number 1 on the blank space next to the first thing you think is appropriate to do in a romantic relationship, number 2 for the next thing, and so forth.

_____ Saying "I love you"

_____ Holding hands

_____ Having sexual intercourse

_____ Introducing the person to your parents

_____ Kissing and making out

_____ Hugging

_____ Getting married

_____ Introducing the person to your friends

_____ Getting naked

_____ Heavy making out with most of your clothes on

_____ Sharing your intimate thoughts and dreams

_____ Slow dancing

_____ Calling the person your "boyfriend" or "girlfriend"

_____ Heavy making out with your clothes off

Is It Love or Infatuation?

What is love and what is infatuation? People often confuse these two. In the blank spaces below indicate whether the statements express love or infatuation.

1. _____ Both people in the relationship think of the other person and his or her needs as well as his or her own needs.

2. _____ One person in the relationship often has to give more than the other person in order for the relationship to work.

3. _____ The relationship is usually based on physical attraction.

4. _____ There is total honesty and trust between the two people in the relationship.

5. _____ Both people accept that the other person is not perfect and they also don't try to change each other.

6. _____ One person may be jealous of the other person's friends and time spent in other activities.

7. _____ Each person is able to be an individual apart from the other. Neither depends totally on the other person for friendship or support.

8. _____ One person realizes that the other is not perfect and so he or she tries to change him or her.

9. _____ During difficult times, this couple remains as committed as during the good times.

10. _____ The two people are close friends, and although they share a physical attraction, this is only one part of their relationship.

11. _____ The relationship is so intense that the two people only spend time with each other and begin to shut out other relationships.

12. _____ This relationship developed slowly, and it took a while for both people to feel they knew and loved the other person.

Love Quotations

Here are some quotations people have made about love. For each quotation, explain in your own words what the person is saying and also whether or not you agree with this view. (Use the back of this sheet if you need more space for answers.)

1. "At the touch of love everyone becomes a poet."
   —Plato

   _____

   _____

2. "Doubt that the stars are fire, doubt that the sun doth move, doubt truth to be a liar, but never doubt love."
   —William Shakespeare

   _____

   _____

3. "Love does not consist of gazing at each other, but in looking together in the same direction."
   —Antoine de Saint-Exupéry

   _____

   _____

4. "'Tis better to have loved and lost than never to have loved at all."
   —Alfred Lord Tennyson

   _____

   _____

5. "We are afraid to care too much, for fear that the other person does not care at all."
   —Eleanor Roosevelt

   _____

   _____

6. "Love is a great beautifier."
   —Louisa May Alcott

   _____

   _____

NAME _____   DATE _____

Sternberg's Love Triangle Theory:
Worksheet 1

Robert Sternberg, a psychologist at Yale University, has done considerable research on love and the various types of love. In his research, he has identified eight types of love using eight triangles. Sternberg believes that ideal love requires three elements: passion, intimacy, and commitment. The ideal or complete love, which he calls consummate love, consists of an isometric triangle with all three elements of love accounted for. The other seven triangles are variations of this complete love.

Below is a triangle that shows consummate love. In the space provided, use a dictionary and your own knowledge of the words to create definitions for the three elements of this kind of love.

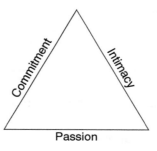

Passion: _____

_____

_____

Intimacy: _____

_____

_____

Commitment: _____

_____

_____

NAME _____   DATE

Sternberg's Love Triangle Theory:
Worksheet 2

Here are the eight types of love according to Sternberg. For each type, write the name of a couple (from either your life, fiction, TV, or film) who exemplify the particular type of love mentioned.

1. **Nonlove**
   (lacks all three elements)

   Couple: _____
   _____

5. **Infatuation**
   (has passion, but lacks commitment and intimacy)

   Couple: _____
   _____

2. **Romantic love**
   (has intimacy and passion, but lacks commitment)

   Couple: _____
   _____

6. **Companionate love**
   (has commitment and intimacy, but lacks passion)

   Couple: _____
   _____

3. **Liking**
   (has intimacy, but lacks commitment and passion)

   Couple: _____
   _____

7. **Empty love**
   (has commitment, but lacks intimacy and passion)

   Couple: _____
   _____

4. **Fatuous love**
   (has commitment and passion, but lacks intimacy)

   Couple: _____
   _____

8. **Consummate love**
   (has all three elements)

   Couple: _____
   _____

Sternberg's Love Triangle Theory:
Worksheet 3

Read the following scenarios. Each scenario describes one of the eight types of love in Sternberg's love triangle theory. Identify the type of love described in each scenario.

1. Ralph and Joyce both lost their spouses to cancer ten years ago. Neither of them desires to remarry, but they both desire companionship. For the past eight years, they have gone on trips together, accompanied each other at family functions, and gone to the theater together. They have never had sex or even kissed, but they also don't date anyone else.

What type of love is this? _____

2. Jillian and Dylan are not dating, but they work in the same office and a few times after work they have met at a hotel and had sex. They have no desire for a relationship because both are dealing with the pains of divorce. However, they are sexually attracted to each other.

What type of love is this? _____

3. Carson and Evelyn have been married for 38 years. They were originally madly in love, but the passion died years ago. They also talk and share their secrets more with their friends than with each other. The marriage isn't great, but both take their vows seriously and are committed to staying together.

What type of love is this? _____

4. Duke and Lara have only dated for three weeks, but they've already told each other all the intimate details of their lives. They also are extremely attracted to each other and can't keep their hands off each other.

What type of love is this? _____

5. Jessica took the bus home for the holidays. On the bus, she sat next to Lance. They hit it off immediately and told each other all their innermost secrets during the six-hour trip. After Jessica arrived at her stop, she never saw Lance again.

What type of love is this? _____

6. Kendra and Ken have been married for seven years. They still enjoy sex on a regular basis. The only problem that Kendra has is that she finds it easier to open up to her friends than to Ken. She has more talks with her girlfriends about her thoughts and feelings than she has with her husband.

What type of love is this? _____

7. Jason and Joan are meeting for the first time in 16 years at their daughter's wedding. They divorced when their daughter was 15 and have not spoken to or seen each other since.

What type of love is this? _____

8. Friends tease Wanda and Robert about having the ideal marriage. After 16 years of marriage, they still find the other attractive. They are also best friends who tell each other everything.

What type of love is this? _____

NAME   DATE

What Type of Lover Are You?

Answer yes or no to each question to determine what type of lover you are. Answer yes if this is one of the qualities you possess in a romantic relationship. Answer no if this is one of the qualities you do not possess. If you are not currently in a relationship, then think of how you acted in past relationships or how you think you might act in a relationship. Note that it is possible to be various types of lovers in a relationship.

1. Type of Lover: The Jealous Type

YES or NO: Do you get jealous when your boyfriend or girlfriend is friendly with someone else of the opposite sex?

2. Type of Lover: The Romantic Type

YES or NO: Are you the type of lover who loves doing romantic things for your boyfriend or girlfriend, such as sneaking kisses, holding hands, and writing romantic notes?

3. Type of Lover: The Egotistical Type

YES or NO: Are you the type of lover who demands the other person think more about your needs than his or her own needs?

4. Type of Lover: The Materialistic Type

YES or NO: Are you the type of lover who likes your boyfriend or girlfriend to express his or her love by showering you with gifts?

5. Type of Lover: The Maniac Type

YES or NO: Do you get so obsessed in a relationship that you become upset if you don't see or hear from your boyfriend or girlfriend every day?

6. Type of Lover: The Pragmatic Type

YES or NO: In a relationship, do you avoid rushing into things until you are sure about your feelings for the other person and that person's feelings for you?

7. Type of Lover: The Companion Type

YES or NO: Do you enjoy being in a relationship where you tell each other everything, are completely honest, and enjoy spending time together?

NAME   DATE

What Matters to You?

Read the statements below. If you believe the statement describes something that is important for you to find in a spouse, then circle 1. If it is sometimes important, circle 2. And if it doesn't matter to you at all, circle 3.

It is important to you that your spouse . . .

	Important	Somewhat Important	Doesn't Matter
Speaks proper English	1	2	3
Spends lots of money on you and showers you with gifts	1	2	3
Remembers every birthday and anniversary	1	2	3
Has proper table manners	1	2	3
Tells you regularly that he/she loves you	1	2	3
Dresses well	1	2	3
Smells good	1	2	3
Has lots of friends	1	2	3
Is in shape and has a fit body	1	2	3
Spends all his/her spare time with you	1	2	3
Tells you regularly that you are attractive	1	2	3
Treats his/her friends and family well and with respect	1	2	3
Enjoys discussing your relationship	1	2	3

NAME _____   DATE

Qualities You Seek in a Mate

Most people fantasize about the person with whom they would like to share their lives. Think of your ideal mate. Rearrange the qualities below in order from 1 to 15. Number 1 means this quality is very important for you to have in a mate and number 15 means this quality is unimportant.

_____You share the same religious beliefs.

_____You are of the same race and cultural background.

_____You share the same interests and enjoy doing things together.

_____You get along with his or her family, and he or she gets along with yours.

_____You have the same friends.

_____You find him or her physically attractive.

_____ He or she is as experienced sexually as you are.

_____ He or she has a good job and makes a specific income.

_____You have similar personalities.

_____You feel a passionate love for each other.

_____You have similar goals and hopes for the future.

_____ He or she has not been married before.

_____You both have similar educational backgrounds.

_____Your desires about children and raising a family are the same.

_____ His or her family gets along with your family.

To Live Together
or Not to Live Together

Many couples today choose to live together before getting married. Statistics, however, do not show that living together means a marriage will be more successful than if a couple doesn't live together. Answer the following questions with your thoughts on this subject.

1. Why do you think people live together before getting married? _____

   _____

   _____

2. Why do you think people choose not to live together before marriage? _____

   _____

   _____

3. What are the advantages and disadvantages of living together before marriage?

Advantages	Disadvantages

4. What are the advantages and disadvantages of not living together before marriage?

Advantages	Disadvantages

5. Would you be open to living with a person before marriage or not? Explain your reasons on the back of this sheet.

Marriage Quotations

Here are some quotations about marriage from some famous people. For each quotation, explain in your own words what the person is saying and also whether or not you agree with this view of marriage.

1. "Marriage is the highest state of friendship."
   —Samuel Richardson

   _____

   _____

2. "Love without marriage can sometimes be very awkward for all concerned; but marriage without love simply removes that institution from the territory of the humanly admissible, to my mind."
   —Katherine Anne Porter

   _____

   _____

3. "A successful marriage is an edifice that must be rebuilt every day."
   —André Maurois

   _____

   _____

4. "Happiness in marriage is entirely a matter of chance."
   —Jane Austen

   _____

   _____

5. "Marriage is one long conversation, chequered by disputes."
   —Robert Louis Stevenson

   _____

   _____

6. "Many a man in love with a dimple make the mistake of marrying the whole girl."
   —Stephen Leacock

   _____

   _____

NAME   DATE

Marriage Vows

Here is a copy of the marriage vows from a Protestant church. A number of couples today are choosing to write their own marriage vows instead of using the traditional ones. In the space provided, write your own version of the marriage vows that highlights what is important to you.

> In the presence of God and before these witnesses,
>
> I, _____, take you, _____,
>   *Christian name*   *Christian name*
>
> to be my husband/wife to have and to hold from this day forward; for better, for worse; for richer, for poorer; in sickness and in health; in joy and in sorrow; to love and to cherish and to be faithful to you alone, as long as we both shall live.

Now it's your turn. Write your marriage vows in the space provided. (Continue on the back of this sheet, if necessary.)

_____

_____

_____

_____

_____

_____

_____

_____

_____

_____

_____

A Marriage Check-off List

Think of a successfully married couple whom you know well. This couple might be your parents or guardians, grandparents, an aunt and uncle, or neighbors. Complete this chart with their marriage in mind.

Name of the Couple _____

	Always	Sometimes	Never
Do they communicate effectively?			
Do they respect each other?			
Do they have fun together?			
Are they committed to the marriage?			
Do they both make compromises?			
Are they friends with each other?			
Do they love each other?			
Do they appear to be attracted to each other?			

What do you think makes their marriage successful?

_____

_____

_____

What can you learn from their marriage?

_____

_____

_____

_____

How Expensive Is It?

Imagine that you got married yesterday. You and your spouse have no car, no furniture, no place to live. Use the classified ads below to pick out everything you'll need. You have $1,000 saved, and you recently quit high school to take a job at $300 a week. Your spouse still attends high school full-time and makes $100 a week at a part-time job. Determine how much you make per year and calculate how much you spend getting settled. Keep in mind, too, that this exercise does not include the amount of money you will spend on food, clothes, entertainment, and so on.

Put a check mark in the box for each item that you choose to purchase.

Bachelor apartment. One large room with a kitchenette, bathroom & shower. Utilities incl. $300/month		Large one bedroom apt. for rent. (heat & water not incl. approx. $50/month) Building has a pool and sauna. $550/month		Two-bedroom luxury apt. All inclusive. Pool, sauna, hot tub, billiard room, and underground parking. $800/month	
10-year-old Honda Civic for sale $5,000.00 o.b.o.		1-year-old Toyota Echo for sale $12,500		Double bed—box spring and mattress $400.00	
King-sized bed—oak— almost brand new $2,500		Double bed mattress $100.00		3 dressers $50.00 each	
TV—$200.00		2 Bookshelves $25/each		Desk and chair $300.00	
Dishes—4 dinner plates, 4 bowls, 4 salad plates, 4 glasses, 4 knives, forks, spoons $200.00		Moving sale—four chairs ($20.00/chair) and one kitchen table ($100), love seat ($200), rocking chair ($75), TV stand ($50)		Couch and matching love seat ($1,000) for the pair. Matching chair ($250)	
coffee table ($50)		2 End tables ($25/each)		VCR ($50)	
Plants, plants, and more plants $5.00 each plant		Lamps—floor lamp $50 two table lamps $25/each 1 reading lamp $10		Used computer and printer $1,000.00	
Oak dining room suite (6 chairs and table) $3,000		Used microwave ($30)		Microwave stand ($50)	
CD stand ($20)		CD player ($150.00)		Big screen TV $1,000	

What is the total amount that you spent? _____

How much will you and your spouse earn in a year? _____

How much will you have left after all the purchases and the rent are paid? _____

Which items did you decide against in order to save money?

_____

_____

87

NAME DATE

Talk-Show Marriage Talk

Imagine that it is 35 years from today and you, as a person successfully married for 25 years, are a rare breed. Pretend you are a guest on a talk show that is focusing on what makes a marriage successful. Answer the host's questions, listed below, as you honestly think you might answer them if you'd been happily married for 25 years.

1. What is the main thing you like about being married? _____
_____

2. What does it take to have a successful marriage? _____
_____
_____

3. With the divorce rate so high, what do you think some couples are not doing to keep their marriages strong?
_____
_____

4. How did having children change your marriage? _____
_____
_____

5. What stresses or difficulties have you dealt with in your marriage? _____
_____
_____

6. How did you successfully overcome these stresses? _____
_____
_____

7. How do you keep your own individuality while working as a team? _____
_____
_____

Copyright © 2004 by John Wiley & Sons, Inc.

NAME _____   DATE _____

Can These Marriages Be Saved?

You are a marriage counselor and the three scenarios below are summaries of your patients' files. For each case, answer (on a separate piece of paper) the following questions:

1. What is the main problem for this married couple?

2. Do you think this marriage can be saved?

3. What advice would you give this couple?

Scenario I

Judy and Rudy became parents of twins just three months ago. Rudy took two weeks off from work after the twins were born and then he went back to work. Unfortunately, Rudy's job involves an hour-and-a-half commute there and back, so he leaves home early and comes home late. Rudy never had siblings and is awkward around the babies. As a result, he avoids holding the twins, changing diapers, and so on. Judy feels that she's doing the work for two. She is exhausted with having the twins and misses working and seeing her friends. She and Rudy have fought nonstop since the birth of the twins, and Judy worries that the marriage is in jeopardy.

Scenario II

Eduardo and Elsie have been married for one year. They did not live together before marriage and only dated for a year before the wedding. As a result of Eduardo's cultural background, he believes that a wife should take care of all the housework and cooking. Elsie does not want to be that kind of wife. Eduardo has threatened that he will not have any children with her unless she becomes the type of wife that he wants. As a result, he has punished her by not having sexual relations with her for the last six months. Elsie loves the Eduardo whom she fell in love with before marriage. Before marriage, Eduardo never told her that this was the type of wife that he wanted her to become. Now that she is married, Elsie refuses to become the type of wife Eduardo wants.

Scenario III

Boris and Rosie have been married for 25 years. Recently their only child, Kendra, left home to attend college. Boris is stressed about the amount of money it costs to have a child in college. Rosie, on the other hand, loves shopping and is not stressed about Kendra's tuition fees. Boris has asked her to stop spending so much money, but that only gets Rosie's back up. Since she earns her own money, she doesn't want Boris to dictate how she spends it. Boris also was approached at work with an early retirement package. He loves his job and is not ready to retire, but if he doesn't accept the package, he may lose his job. Boris and Rosie are fighting for the first time in their marriage and their money problems do not seem to be going away.

Why Do Relationships End?

Unfortunately, with the divorce rate hovering around 50 percent, many marriages end. Even when people are in successful marriages, there are lots of stresses. In the chart provided, write down 10 reasons why you think couples may end their relationship. Then, in Column A, put a check mark beside the reasons that you think are legitimate, good reasons for ending a marriage. In Column B, put a check mark beside those that you think are not good reasons for ending a relationship.

	A	B
1.		
2.		
3.		
4.		
5.		
6.		
7.		
8.		
9.		
10.		

Looking at the Family

1. Create a definition for the word *family*. _____

   _____

2. Describe the members of your immediate family. _____

   _____

   _____

   _____

3. What are the benefits of being part of a family? _____

   _____

   _____

   _____

4. What are the stresses or drawbacks involved in being part of a family? _____

   _____

   _____

   _____

5. How do American families differ today from families 200 years ago? _____

   _____

   _____

   _____

6. How do you think the American family might change 100 years from today? _____

   _____

   _____

   _____

   _____

Family Challenges

In today's world, a family does not necessarily consist of a mother, father, and children. Many unique combinations make up a family. In the chart below are descriptions of nontraditional families. Complete the chart by determining some of the challenges these families might face.

Types of Families	Challenges Faced
Single-Parent Family— A child(ren) lives with one parent	
Adoptive Family— A child(ren) is adopted by a couple	
Step Family— After divorce, a couple may remarry and each bring their children from the first marriage into one family	
Homosexual Family— A gay couple live together with a child(ren)	
Teenage Parent— A female gets pregnant in her teens and begins a family	

If Parenthood Required a License . . .

Imagine that a law has been passed requiring people to get licenses before they can become parents. You have been hired to decide who should get licenses and on what basis. Fill in this form to explain who will qualify for a license.

1. Will you have an age stipulation? If no, explain why not. If yes, give the age range and explain why you chose this age range.

   _____

   _____

   _____

   _____

2. Will you have an education requirement? If no, explain why not. If yes, give the educational background required and explain why you chose this.

   _____

   _____

   _____

   _____

3. Will you have financial requirements? If no, explain why not. If yes, give the financial requirements needed and explain why you chose this.

   _____

   _____

   _____

   _____

4. What other requirements, skills, or traits would you require from prospective parents? Explain why you chose these requirements.

   _____

   _____

   _____

   _____

Stages in the Family Life Cycle

In 1973, Jay Haley created a concept he called the family life cycle. The family life cycle describes the stages a traditional couple goes through from getting married, to creating a family, to dealing with aging. Examine Haley's eight stages of the family life cycle. For each stage, try to determine the goals the parents or couple would be trying to attain while in that particular stage. Write these goals in the space provided on the right-hand side of the chart.

Stage	Goals
1. Newly married couple	
2. Starting a family (the eldest child would be less than 30 months old)	
3. Families with preschool children (children's ages range from $2^1/_2$ - 6 years old)	
4. Families with preteens (children's ages range from 6-13 years old)	
5. Families with teens (children's ages range from 13-20)	
6. Families with young adults (the eldest may have left home and the youngest is getting ready to leave)	
7. Post-parenting couples (all children have left home)	
8. Aging couples (retirement and beyond)	

Who's in What Stage of the Family Life Cycle?

For each couple, indicate the stage they are in according to Jay Haley's family life cycle.

1. Lai-Sheung and her husband, Ty, are up to their eyeballs in diapers. They can't wait until their two sons are toilet-trained. *At what stage in the family life cycle are Lai-Sheung and Ty?* _____

2. Hiroko and Makato are preparing for their eldest daughter's wedding next month. They are also looking forward to the birth of their first grandchild when their son and his wife have a baby in six months. *At what stage in the family life cycle are Hiroko and Makato?* _____

3. Juanita retired from work six months ago and her husband, Isaac, retired six years ago. *At what stage in the family life cycle are Juanita and Isaac?* _____

4. Francesca and Frank have two children: a boy in fourth grade and a girl in sixth grade. *At what stage in the family life cycle are Francesca and Frank?* _____

5. Colette plans to make a special dinner for Oman to celebrate their first-month anniversary of marriage. *At what stage in the family life cycle are Colette and Oman?* _____

6. Donna and Peter are getting their four-year-old twin sons ready for school in the fall by teaching them their ABCs and how to count to 10. *At what stage in the family life cycle are Donna and Peter?* _____

7. Muhammad and Ingrid have a daughter who is newly married and living in Texas and another daughter at home who will leave in the fall to attend college. *At what stage in the family life cycle are Muhammad and Ingrid?* _____

8. Krista and Kris have four kids. The eldest is 19 and the youngest is 14. *At what stage in the family life cycle are Krista and Kris?* _____

LIFE SKILLS

Life is change; growth is optional.

Karen Kaiser Clark

NAME _____   DATE

Maslow's Hierarchy of Needs

People have various needs. We need shelter, and we need love. Dr. Abraham Maslow, a psychologist, created what he called Maslow's Needs Hierarchy, which arranges the needs of all people in a hierarchy of importance from the most important basic needs (physical needs) on up. Below is a summary of Maslow's Needs Hierarchy. Read this and then determine the needs of the people in the exercise below.

1. Deidra plans to study hard in math, so she can win the math award in school.

What are her needs? _____

2. Jason's best friend has stopped speaking to Jason, and Jason is not sure what he has done wrong.

What are his needs? _____

3. The Wong family lost their house in a fire and plan to build a new one.

What are their needs? _____

4. A dog chases a little boy, and the boy screams for help from his parents.

What are his needs? _____

5. A woman takes acting lessons and auditions for a play so that she can fulfill her lifetime desire of becoming an actress.

What are her needs? _____

Maslow's Needs and You

Think of Maslow's Needs Hierarchy. How can you ensure that your needs in the five areas are met? Look at this chart and determine how your needs are met in each section. Then write your answers on a separate sheet of paper.

Self-Fulfillment Needs
What do you do to meet your self-fulfillment needs?

Self-Worth Needs
What do you do to meet your self-worth needs?

Love and Friendship Needs
What do you do to meet your love and friendship needs?

Safety Needs
How are your safety needs met?

Physical Needs
How are your physical needs met?

NAME _____ DATE _____

A Goal Chart

People have goals in various areas. They may have career goals, relationship goals, education goals, financial goals, and health goals. A health goal, for example, may be to give up smoking, while a career goal may be to become a partner in a law firm and make $500,000 a year. Goals also change over time. Fill in this chart by indicating your 5-year, 10-year, and 20-year goals in each area. You may wish to keep this chart and see what comes true in 20 years.

Types of Goals	Five Years You will be age _____	Ten Years You will be age _____	Twenty Years You will be age _____
Education Goals			
Career Goals			
Relationship and Family Goals			
Financial Goals			
Health and Fitness Goals			

High and Low Self-Esteem

Having high self-esteem is a positive life skill. People with low self-esteem tend to get into drugs, deal with many disorders, and find themselves in unhealthy situations.

Below is a list of statements. If the statement describes a characteristic of someone with low self-esteem, put a check mark in the column entitled LOW. If the statement describes a characteristic of someone with high self-esteem, put a check mark in the column entitled HIGH. If you believe the statement describes your attitude toward yourself, then also put a check mark in the column entitled YOU. Do you have more check marks in the low self-esteem category or in the high self-esteem category?

	LOW	HIGH	YOU
1. Fears change or trying new things			
2. Takes responsibility for one's actions and mistakes			
3. Able to take charge and show leadership when necessary			
4. Brags about accomplishments and needs to be the center of attention			
5. Aware and accepting of one's own strengths and weaknesses			
6. Unable to show leadership and tends to follow others			
7. When victimized remains a victim and does not overcome the situation			
8. Accepts change and is eager to try new things			
9. Has self-respect and self-confidence			
10. Always criticizes self or finds blame in others			
11. Gets approval from self and does not depend on approval from others			
12. Tends to find the negative in things, people, and situations			

NAME DATE

Improving Your Self-Esteem

The following is a list of ways to improve your self-esteem. For each suggestion there is a short exercise for you to complete. Complete the exercise in the space provided.

You can improve your self-esteem by. . . .

1. Recognizing your talents. Write down five of your talents.

   a. _____

   b. _____

   c. _____

   d. _____

   e. _____

2. Taking care of your physical, mental, and emotional self. Explain in a sentence how you take care of each.

   a. Physical self: _____

   b. Mental self: _____

   c. Emotional self: _____

3. Setting realistic and attainable goals. List three of your realistic and attainable goals.

   a. _____

   b. _____

   c. _____

4. Building a network of good friends who are positive influences in your life. List the names of your close network of friends.

   _____

5. Understanding the positive contributions you make in your family. Explain in a few sentences the positive contributions you make in your family.

   _____

   _____

   _____

Peer Pressure and You

Complete the following sentences so that your response helps define the term "peer pressure" and how it affects you.

In my opinion, peer pressure can be defined as _____

_____

Peer pressure exists in the following places: _____

_____

One time that I did not succumb to peer pressure was when _____

_____

_____

_____

One example of when I succumbed to peer pressure was when _____

_____

_____

_____

One example of when I pressured a peer was when _____

_____

_____

_____

My attitude toward peer pressure is _____

_____

_____

Learning Assertiveness

Throughout life, an assertive person communicates his or her needs and desires more effectively than a passive or aggressive person. Using the dictionary (or drawing on your own knowledge), create a definition for passive, aggressive, and assertive.

Passive: _____

Aggressive: _____

Assertive: _____

In the statements provided below, determine if each statement is assertive, passive, or aggressive.

1. _____ "You're a fool if you think you can make the swim team."

2. _____ "I think you will benefit more from trying the homework questions yourself than from copying my homework."

3. _____ "I'm sorry. It's probably my fault that you're in a bad mood."

4. _____ "I don't think that we should be drinking a bottle of beer, but if we don't tell anyone, hopefully our parents won't catch us."

5. _____ "If you don't come to the party, I'll tell everyone what a lame loser you are."

6. _____ "I don't want to see a movie; I would rather do something more active because I've been sitting all day."

For the situation below, write a passive, an aggressive, and an assertive response.

> Your friends are trying to persuade you to have a party at your place on a weekend when your parents are away. You know that your parents would not approve of you having this party.

The passive response: _____

_____

The aggressive response: _____

_____

The assertive response: _____

_____

NAME   DATE

More on Assertiveness

Put a check mark next to the sentences that describe how an assertive person reacts. Then write the word *passive* or *aggressive* at the end of the other statements to indicate if the reaction describes a passive or aggressive response.

_____You look the person directly in the eyes.

_____You acknowledge the other person's feelings but also offer an explanation for your own feelings.

_____You raise your voice and yell at the person.

_____You make sure your voice is strong with a confident tone.

_____You use sarcasm and put-downs.

_____You make sure that your facial expressions always match what you're saying.

_____You use "I" statements whenever possible.

_____You whisper or mumble.

_____You are confident in what you are saying and aren't afraid to take a stand.

_____You stand as close as possible to the person you are addressing.

_____You show that you are embarrassed or uncomfortable whenever someone compliments you.

_____You apologize even if you didn't do anything wrong.

NAME

DATE

Dealing with Difficult People

We all encounter difficult people in our lives. Here are some descriptions of difficult people. In the space provided, jot down some positive ways of dealing with each type of person.

1. **Show-offs:** These people must be the center of attention whenever possible.

   _____

   _____

2. **Worriers:** These people worry about everything and expect the worst.

   _____

   _____

3. **Gossipers:** These people spread rumors and often exaggerate information.

   _____

   _____

4. **Guilt-trippers:** These people put others on guilt trips in order to get them to do certain things.

   _____

   _____

5. **Bullies:** These people use threats, fear, and cruelty to control others.

   _____

   _____

6. **Whiners:** These people grumble and complain about everything.

   _____

   _____

7. **Know-it-alls:** These people act like they know everything.

   _____

   _____

Conflict Outcomes

When two parties are involved in a conflict, there are four potential outcomes.

- **Avoidance:** This occurs when one of the parties walks away from the issue, making the other party an automatic winner in the conflict. In this case, there is a definite winner and loser.
- **Passivity and dominance:** This is when one party passively gives up, allowing the other party to win by default. As in avoidance, there is a definite winner and loser.
- **Compromise:** In this situation, both parties compromise and give up something in order to solve the conflict. In this case, no one wins and no one loses.
- **Collaborative problem solving:** In this case, both sides, usually with the help of a mediator, come up with a mutually acceptable solution. As with a compromise, there is no winner and no loser in this case.

For each case below, determine which of the four methods is the conflict outcome, and write the name of that outcome in the space provided.

1. _____ Amanda and her brother, Bruce, are always fighting over the car that they share. Amanda is upset because Bruce has had the car for the last three weekends. Finally, the siblings sit down with their mom and come up with a schedule that gives Amanda the car from Wednesday to Friday night, and Bruce the car from Saturday morning to Tuesday night. The second week, Amanda gets the car from Saturday to Tuesday, and Bruce gets it from Wednesday to Friday.

2. _____ Duncan challenges Omar to a fight after school because Omar secretly went on a date with Duncan's girlfriend. Omar leaves school early and races home so that he doesn't have to fight Duncan.

3. _____ Eric wants Natasha's shift at work, so he changes the schedule without asking Natasha. Natasha is upset about the switch because she'd made plans according to the schedule. However, she doesn't say anything to Eric because he's the boss's son, and she simply accepts the new schedule and changes her plans.

4. _____ Misha and her mom have gotten into a fight about Misha's grades. Misha's mom doesn't think that Misha spends enough time concentrating on school and spends too much time with her friends. Misha and her mom come up with an arrangement that Misha will only go out with her friends one night a week until her report card comes out. Then, if her marks have improved by at least 10 percent, Misha can go out three nights a week with her friends.

NAME   DATE

The Steps in Decision Making

There are five steps in the decision-making process. Examine each step in Column A, then use Column B to illustrate how you put that step into practice through a recent decision in your own life.

COLUMN A	COLUMN B - Your Examples
Step 1 - Identify the problem.	
Step 2 - Look at all the choices you can make in terms of a course of action.	
Step 3 - Consider the pros and cons of each of your options.	
Step 4 - Choose a course of action and act upon it.	
Step 5 - Evaluate the results.	

Good Leader, Weak Leader (Part 1)

This exercise contrasts the qualities between good leaders and weak leaders. Think of three good leaders who fit the criteria mentioned below. Write the name of each leader in the appropriate space and then brainstorm all the qualities that make these people good leaders.

1. A good leader of a sports team—Name the leader: _____

   List the qualities that make him or her a good leader: _____

   _____

2. A good leader in your school or community—Name the leader: _____

   List the qualities that make him or her a good leader: _____

   _____

3. A good political leader—Name the leader: _____

   List the qualities that make him or her a good leader: _____

   _____

Now think of three weak leaders who fit the criteria mentioned below. Write the name of each leader in the appropriate space provided and then brainstorm all the things that make these people weak leaders.

1. A weak leader of a sports team—Name the leader: _____

   List the qualities that make him or her a weak leader: _____

   _____

2. A weak leader in your community—Name the leader: _____

   List the qualities that make him or her a weak leader: _____

   _____

3. A weak political leader—Name the leader: _____

   List the qualities that make him or her a weak leader: _____

   _____

Good Leader, Weak Leader (Part 2)

Using the information that you gathered on the first page of this worksheet, complete this chart by listing five qualities of good leaders and five qualities of weak leaders.

Qualities of Good Leaders	Qualities of Weak Leaders
1.	
2.	
3.	
4.	
5.	

Wawa Island:
A Team-Building Activity

Until recently, Wawa Island, a small desolate island 50 miles long and 4 miles wide off the coast of Florida, was owned by a billionaire named John Johnston III. When Mr. Johnston passed away recently, he left a strange will, leaving the uninhabited island to five individuals who will move there and create a new country. Mr. Johnston left the choosing of the five people to a committee.

Your teacher will divide you into small groups of five or six. Your group is the committee of people who must choose the new citizens of Wawa Island. Read the list of applicants below and on the next sheet, and then decide which five people will move there. Make sure that each member of the group has input.

After the exercise, evaluate your team. Did you work as a group? Did anyone dominate or did everyone get an equal say?

The Wawa Island Applicants

1. **Maher Sharawi:** male, age 27. Maher currently works as a chef at a five-star restaurant. He has never been married, but did father a child when he was in his late teens.

2. **Stephanie De Luca:** female, age 21. Stephanie is a plumber by trade who does electrical work on the side. She also speaks three languages.

3. **Kesha and Patrick Shaw:** female and male, ages 37 and 40, respectively. Kesha is a medical doctor and her husband, Patrick, is a high school physical education teacher. They will only move to Wawa Island on the condition that they can go together. Patrick was diagnosed with cancer three years ago, but it is in remission.

4. **Joan Tran:** female, age 56. One of Joan's novels won the Pulitzer Prize for literature. Joan is a full-time writer who has also competed in triathlons over the past 20 years.

5. **Austin Crawford:** male, age 40. Crawford owns his own construction company. He is recently divorced and wants to start a new life.

6. **Grant Mathies:** male, age 19. Although Grant dropped out of high school at age 16, he is a computer whiz who was hired by IBM two years ago to build software. He's already a millionaire.

7. **Effy Papadopolous:** female, age 32. Effy lives in New York City but works all over the world. She's a talented businesswoman specializing in international trade.

NAME   DATE

8. **Antero da Silva:** male, age 32. Antero recently retired from the NFL and wants a new challenge. He also acted in a few Hollywood movies when he was in his early twenties.

9. **Jennifer Moore:** female, age 58. Jennifer's current job is as a professional gardener. However, three years ago she retired from banking, where she worked as an executive in one of America's largest banks.

10. **Noah Ambrose:** male, age 31. Most people address Noah as "Father" because he is a Catholic priest.

11. **Chad Henry:** male, age 42. Chad worked as a lawyer until he became a politician three years ago.

12. **Joe Francovic:** male, age 63. Joe is a retired farmer who also built a house by himself.

13. **Libby Campbell:** female, age 21. Libby is a model who also works as a cheerleader for an NFL team.

14. **Julie Wells:** female, age 28. Julie owns three successful fast-food restaurants and teaches aerobics at night.

NAME   DATE

Are You an Effective Communicator?

How well do you communicate with others? For each of the following statements, circle 1, 2, or 3 depending on how effectively you communicate with people.

	Never/Rarely	Sometimes	Always
1. You make eye contact during conversations.	1	2	3
2. You show you are listening to what the other person is saying by nodding and gesturing.	1	2	3
3. You avoid interrupting the other person before he or she has finished talking.	1	2	3
4. You ask probing questions that demonstrate your interest in what the other person is saying.	1	2	3
5. Your voice is clear and can easily be heard and understood by people.	1	2	3
6. You observe nonverbal cues from the other person.	1	2	3
7. You make sure a conversation involves both people and isn't just you doing all of the talking or listening.	1	2	3
8. You compliment people.	1	2	3
9. You avoid negative nonverbal signs, such as yawning, even if the conversation isn't interesting.	1	2	3
10. You ask for clarification if you are unsure about what the other person is saying.	1	2	3

- If you got a score of 25 or higher, then you are an excellent communicator.

- If you got a score of 16 to 24, then you are an effective communicator.

- If your score was 15 or less, then you may want to work on your communication skills.

Name That Communication Blocker

Communication blockers are comments that prevent good communication from occurring. Following is a list of some communication blockers. Below the list are some comments. For each comment, identify the type of communication blocker that is being illustrated.

Communication Blockers

Preaching: Telling the person what he or she should do.

Blaming: Blaming the person for the situation he or she is in.

Diverting: Changing the conversation to another topic.

Ordering: Ordering the person to do something or act in a certain manner.

Ridiculing: Name-calling, or making fun of the person.

---

1. "You're such a jerk sometimes." _____

2. "I believe it is your responsibility to marry Karen since you got her pregnant."

   _____

3. "It's all your fault because you always try to ruin everything."

   _____

4. "You go and talk to Mom, or else." _____

5. "I'm tired of always analyzing our relationship. Let's talk about something else."

   _____

6. "If you hadn't lied in the first place, you would not be in this situation now."

   _____

7. "I can't believe how stupid you are." _____

8. "Let's talk later. I don't have time right now." _____

9. "You must see him tonight and tell him it's over." _____

10. "In this situation the only thing that you can do is ask for forgiveness."

   _____

NAME _____   DATE

Techniques for Saying No

Throughout life, you are likely to meet people who will attempt to convince you to do things you don't want to do. Below are different refusal techniques and an example of each one. In the final column, provide your own example of each technique.

Name of the Technique	Example	Your Example
Just Say No	Person A - "Do you want to smoke a cigarette?" Person B - "No thanks."	
Give a Reason	Person A - "Do you want to have sex?" Person B - "No thanks. I'm waiting until I'm married."	
Walk Away or Avoid the Situation	If you know that Dave always has drugs at his parties and you don't want to do drugs or feel comfortable around them, then just don't go to his parties.	
Change the Subject	Person A - "Do you want to go to my car and make out?" Person B - "Let's dance to this song. I love this song."	
Reverse the Pressure	Person A - "Do you want to smoke a joint?" Person B - "I don't need to do drugs to prove that I'm cool."	
Delay	Person A - "Do you want to start dating?" Person B - "Let's be friends for a while and wait until we know each other better."	

Communication Scenarios

How would you help the following people communicate in the following situations? Write your responses in the spaces provided.

1. A new student who can't speak a word of English joins your Phys. Ed. class. His family just fled their native country, and he's having a difficult time adjusting. You have been asked by your Phys. Ed. teacher to show this student around and help him fit in. How do you communicate when you have a language barrier?

    _____

    _____

    _____

    _____

    _____

2. You have made friends with someone who is hearing impaired. Another friend of yours is having a party and you invite your hearing-impaired friend to go with you. How do you help your friend communicate and meet your other friends at the party?

    _____

    _____

    _____

    _____

3. Your two closest friends aren't speaking to each other. The three of you were inseparable until the other two got into a fight. How do you get your friends to communicate with each other and stop fighting?

    _____

    _____

    _____

    _____

    _____

What Are They Really Saying?

Much of what we communicate is expressed through nonverbal gestures. For example, our body language and gestures can say we're bored even though our words may be saying something else.

The following list describes nonverbal gestures. In the column on the right, indicate what message these gestures might give you if the person you are communicating with did this while you were having a conversation.

Gesture	Message Given
1. A Smile	
2. Rolling the Eyes	
3. A Yawn	
4. Waving the Index Finger in the Air	
5. Tapping the Foot	
6. Laughing	
7. Rubbing the Eyes	
8. Dropping the Jaw and Exposing a Wide Open Mouth	
9. Shrugging the Shoulders	
10. Crossing the Arms	

113

A Paired Listening Exercise:
Teacher Page

This exercise is designed to help students work on their listening skills. For this exercise, arrange the class into pairs and have them sit about five feet apart from their partner. Give one partner Script A and the other partner Script B. The two scripts tell the same story, except Script A is missing words that are in Script B, and Script B is missing words that are in Script A.

The two partners should read the scripts in unison. When the person with Script A comes to a blank space in his script, he listens for the word that goes into the blank from the person with Script B and then quickly writes the word in the blank space. And when the person with Script B comes to a blank space in her script, she listens for the word that goes into the blank space from the person with Script A and quickly writes the word in the blank space. The goal is to see which pair can finish first and have the two scripts filled in correctly.

A word of warning: This exercise can get rather noisy.

Answers: Juanita and Zana were taking a shortcut through the woods when suddenly they saw a bear. Juanita screamed, "Climb a tree and make lots of noise." Before Zana could count to three, Juanita had climbed a tree and was screaming. Meanwhile, Zana panicked. She could not find a tree to climb. One tree looked too skinny. The other trees' branches were too thin. Finally, Zana climbed on top of a tree stump. She looked at the bear and the bear looked at her. She knew she had to make some noise and began singing "I'm a Little Teapot" at the top of her lungs and doing the actions to the song as she stood on the stump. The bear stood on its hind legs and looked at Zana. After a few minutes, it wandered away. The girls were safe, but Juanita stayed in the tree laughing for an hour.

NAME _____   DATE

A Paired Listening Exercise:
Student Page, Script A

Juanita and _____ were taking a _____ cut through _____ woods when

_____ they saw a _____. Juanita _____, "Climb a

_____ and make lots of _____." Before _____ could count to

_____, Juanita had _____ a tree and was _____. Meanwhile, Zana

_____. She could not _____ a tree to _____. One _____

looked too _____. The other _____ branches were too _____. Finally,

Zana _____ on top of a _____ stump. She _____ at the bear

and the _____ looked at _____. She _____ she had to

_____ some _____ and began singing "_____ a Little

_____" at the top of _____ lungs and _____ the actions to the

_____ as she _____ on the stump. The _____ stood on _____

hind _____ and looked at _____. After a _____ minutes, _____

wandered _____. The girls were _____, but Juanita _____ in the

tree _____ for an hour.

113b

A Paired Listening Exercise:
Student Page, Script B

Juanita and Zana were _____ a short _____ through the _____ when

suddenly they _____ a bear. _____ screamed, "_____ a tree and

_____ lots of noise." _____ Zana could _____ to three, _____

had climbed a _____ and was screaming. _____, Zana panicked. _____

could not find a _____ to climb. _____ tree looked _____ skinny. The

_____ trees' _____ were too thin. Finally, _____ climbed on

_____ of a tree _____. She looked at the _____ and the bear

_____ at her. _____ knew _____ had to make _____ noise and

began _____ "I'm a _____ Teapot" at the _____ of her

_____ and doing the _____ to the song as _____ stood on the

_____. The bear _____ on its _____ legs and _____ at Zana.

_____ a few _____, it _____ away. The _____ were safe,

but _____ stayed in the _____ laughing for an _____.

NAME _____   DATE _____

Help Fatima Manage Her Time (Part 1)

Fatima has difficulty managing her time. Recently her mom recommended that Fatima make to-do lists to help keep her organized. Below is Fatima's list for this Saturday and Sunday. Next to each item is the approximate time each chore or activity will take to complete. For some items, like her job at the bookstore, the exact hours that she is already scheduled for are listed. Read this list and then complete the tasks that follow.

Fatima's To-Do List

_____ Work at the bookstore (4 hrs. Saturday from 9 to 1; 5 hrs. Sunday from 1 to 6)

_____ Swim laps at the pool (1 hr.)

_____ Meet Luba for coffee (1 hr.)

_____ Do research at the library for a school project that's due in three weeks (2 hrs.)

_____ Baby-sit for the Chow family on Saturday night (4 hrs. from 6 to 10)

_____ Write English essay that's due on Monday morning (5 hrs.)

_____ Go to James's party on Saturday night (3 hrs.)

_____ Do homework for school for Monday's classes (3 hrs.)

_____ Sing in choir at church on Sunday morning and rehearse (2 hrs. from 10 to 12)

_____ Clean bedroom (1 hr.)

_____ Do weekly chores at home (2 hrs.)

_____ Chat with friends in on-line chatroom (2 hrs.)

_____ Pick up Mom at the airport (2 hrs. Saturday from 1 to 3)

_____ Nap (1 hr.)

_____ Search the Internet for places for March break trip (1 hr.)

_____ Go to a movie with Abdi on Sunday night (3 hrs. starting at 7)

It is impossible for Fatima to complete all these activities in the time allotted. Rank the items in order of priority from #1 (most important) to #16 (least important).

Next, in the space below, explain why you organized the tasks in the manner you did. Which tasks will Fatima probably not have time to do? Why would you drop those tasks?

_____

_____

_____

_____

_____

NAME _____   DATE

Help Fatima Manage Her Time (Part 2)

Fill out the day-timer below by scheduling the items from Fatima's list. You will probably decide not to use all of the items because there isn't enough time, so just schedule the items that you feel are of most importance. You do not need to allow time for Fatima to get from place to place since this has already been included in the approximate times. But you will need to schedule in time for Fatima to sleep.

SATURDAY	SUNDAY
6 a.m.	6 a.m.
7 a.m.	7 a.m.
8 a.m.	8 a.m.
9 a.m.	9 a.m.
10 a.m.	10 a.m.
11 a.m.	11 a.m.
12 p.m.	12 p.m.
1 p.m.	1 p.m.
2 p.m.	2 p.m.
3 p.m.	3 p.m.
4 p.m.	4 p.m.
5 p.m.	5 p.m.
6 p.m.	6 p.m.
7 p.m.	7 p.m.
8 p.m.	8 p.m.
9 p.m.	9 p.m.
10 p.m.	10 p.m.
11 p.m.	11 p.m.
12 a.m.	12 a.m.
1 a.m.	1 a.m.
2 a.m.	2 a.m.
3 a.m.	3 a.m.
4 a.m.	4 a.m.
5 a.m.	5 a.m.

NAME _____   DATE _____

Managing Your Time (Part 1)

To-do lists are a great way of organizing your time. Think of the week ahead. In the chart below, brainstorm all of the things you need to complete or do during the week. In Column 2, write down approximately how long the various tasks will take to complete (and the specific day you must complete them by, if there is a specific day). In Column 3, write down an M if this task is something that you must do or a W if this task is something you want to do but don't necessarily have to do. For example, writing a report for your science class is something you must do, whereas meeting your friends at the mall is something you would like to do but don't have to do.

Tasks for the Week	Approx. time & day	M or W

Managing Your Time (Part 2)

Using the items from the worksheet Managing Your Time (Part 1), schedule these items into the weekly calendar below. You may also wish to include the times you will start and finish each item.

Time of Day	Monday	Tuesday	Wednesday
morning			
afternoon			
evening			

Time of Day	Thursday	Friday	Saturday	Sunday
morning				
afternoon				
evening				

NAME
DATE

What Do You Do?

In order to improve your time management skills, it is important to examine how you spend your time. Do you spend too many hours watching TV and not enough hours doing homework? Think about your previous week. Try to remember how many hours you spent doing the activities and tasks mentioned in the chart below. Indicate the number of these hours in the column titled "Time Spent Doing." Then answer the following questions:

1. Do you think this chart demonstrates that you use your time wisely? If not, how could you improve your time management?

   _____

   _____

   _____

2. Does this chart show you anything that you do too much of? What?

   _____

   _____

   _____

3. Does this chart reveal anything that you don't do enough of? What?

   _____

   _____

   _____

	Time Spent Doing		Time Spent Doing
Sleeping		Watching TV	
Eating		At School	
Extracurricular Activities		Watching Movies	
Showering and Dressing		Exercising	
Spending Time on the Computer		Reading	
Homework		Talking on the Phone	
Other:		Other:	
Other:		Other:	

NAME   DATE

Fatima's Errands:
A Time Management Activity

Have you ever found that you went to the bank to cash a check, came back home, and then went back out to the store—which is next to the bank—to pick up some groceries? You could have saved a lot of time by doing both errands at once. The purpose of this time management activity is to teach you to plan ahead and organize yourself when you're out doing things like errands.

Instructions: Below is a map of Fatima's neighborhood, with all the places marked where Fatima needs to go to do errands. Underneath the map is Fatima's to-do list with all the jobs and activities she needs to complete on a Saturday afternoon. Using the map, decide in what order Fatima should do each item on her list. Write 1 in the blank space next to the first activity she should do, 2 next to the second activity, and so on. Ideally, Fatima should complete all these tasks on one trip.

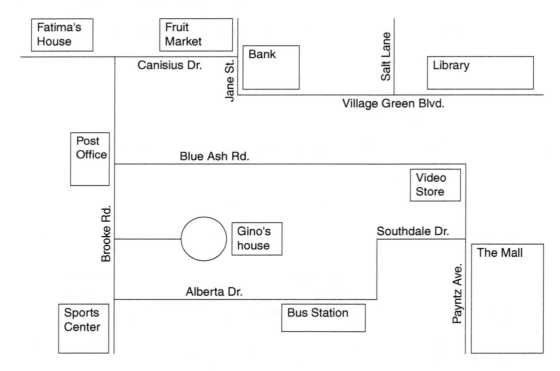

_____ Drop off books at the library.

_____ Buy stamps at the post office.

_____ Buy a birthday card for Lisa at the mall.

_____ Pick up her brother from the bus station.

_____ Cash a check at the bank.

_____ Take a video back to the video store.

_____ Buy a sweater at the mall.

_____ Buy mangos and cantaloupe at the fruit market.

_____ Register for basketball at the sports center.

_____ Drop off the books borrowed from Gino.

Types of Violence

According to Webster's dictionary, violence is a "force used to cause injury or damage and the harm done by lack of proper respect." There are a number of different types of violence. Below is a list of various types of violence. For each one, create a definition and an example that illustrates the definition.

Bullying: _____

_____

_____

_____

Psychological violence: _____

_____

_____

_____

Sexual violence: _____

_____

_____

_____

Physical violence: _____

_____

_____

_____

Is Your School Violent?

Complete the chart below to examine the violence at your school.

At your school, have you witnessed or experienced a problem with . . .

	Never	Rarely	Sometimes	Often
name calling?				
bullying or intimidation?				
sexual harassment?				
racial harassment?				
gang-related violence?				
theft?				
vandalism?				
mistreatment or disrespect toward teachers?				
threats of weapons?				
physical fights?				

Based on this chart, do you think that your school has a violence problem?

_____

_____

How do you think the problem with violence should be addressed, and if possible, changed?

_____

_____

_____

_____

_____

_____

Top 10 Pieces of Advice to Live By

Before dying of cancer, teacher Ron McRae left his sixth-grade class at James McQueen Public School these top 10 pieces of advice to live by. After reading Mr. McRae's advice, create your own top 10 pieces of advice to live by in the space provided.

Ron McRae's Top 10 Pieces of Advice to Live By

1. Don't sweat the small stuff.

2. Listen to your heart and let it tell you what makes it happy.

3. Approach each obstacle as an opportunity.

4. Make every moment count.

5. Never underestimate the importance of family.

6. Never underestimate the power of love.

7. Don't let fear consume you.

8. Don't carry a grudge.

9. Allow some quiet time for yourself each day.

10. Appreciate the magnificence of being you.

Now it's your turn.

Your Top 10 Pieces of Advice to Live By

1. _____

2. _____

3. _____

4. _____

5. _____

6. _____

7. _____

8. _____

9. _____

10. _____

Advice in Code

A wise elder has given you this sheet of paper. "On it," the elder has said, "is the greatest piece of advice I can give you." You need to break the code to reveal these wise words. Here is the only clue the elder has given you: Z = A

WLM'G YV ZUIZRW

GL YV BLFIHVOU

ZMW ULOOLD

BLFI LDM

KZGS

RM

ORUV.

What is the coded message?

_____

_____

_____

SECTION **5**

STRESS

The process of living is the process of reacting to stress.

Dr. Stanley J. Sarnoff

Are You Vulnerable to Stress?

We can't avoid stress; however, some of us are more vulnerable to stress than others. For example, if you are overweight and feel tired all the time, you are more vulnerable to stress than a person who is fit and healthy. Complete this questionnaire and learn how vulnerable you are to stress. Answer each question by circling the response that best suits you. In other words, circle 1 if you always do what is asked and 5 if you never do what is asked. Once you have completed the questionnaire, total your results.

	Always	Often	Sometimes	Rarely	Never
1. Do you eat three balanced meals a day?	1	2	3	4	5
2. Do you usually get seven to eight hours of sleep a night?	1	2	3	4	5
3. Do you exercise for half an hour at least three times a week?	1	2	3	4	5
4. Are you at an appropriate weight for your height?	1	2	3	4	5
5. Do you avoid smoking?	1	2	3	4	5
6. Do you avoid excessive drinking?	1	2	3	4	5
7. Are you healthy overall?	1	2	3	4	5
8. Are you organized and able to manage your time effectively?	1	2	3	4	5
9. Do you have a close friend or family member who lives within a half-hour drive?	1	2	3	4	5
10. Do you socialize with your friends or take part in an organized activity at least twice a week?	1	2	3	4	5

Total score: _____

A score of 15 or less means that you have an excellent resistance to stress. A score of 16 to 30 means that you have a good resistance to stress, but you could improve in a few areas. A score of 31 or above means you have a high vulnerability to stress, and you may wish to modify your lifestyle so that you are better able to cope with stress.

NAME _____   DATE _____

The Life Change Index

In the 1960s, Dr. Thomas Holmes and Dr. Richard Rahe interviewed 7,000 people about the life events they experienced in the course of a year. From this research, they established a life change index. Holmes and Rahe found that people with the highest scores were most likely to develop a stress-induced illness. The index below has been adapted from Dr. Holmes and Dr. Rahe's original index. Place an X in the column labeled "occurred to you" for any events that happened to you in the past 12 months. Then total your score.

Event	Score	Occurred to You
death of a parent	100	
death of a sibling or close family member	95	
parents separated or divorced	90	
an unexpected pregnancy (you got pregnant or got someone pregnant)	85	
in trouble with the law	80	
major personal illness or injury	80	
serious illness of a family member or close friend	75	
death of a close friend	75	
marriage or engagement	70	
breakup of serious relationship or marriage	65	
gained a new family member (through marriage or birth)	64	
sexually molested or raped	64	
moved to new town or state	62	
home broken into or burned	60	
entered college or a new school	60	
change in financial status (yours or your parents')	58	
problems with friends	55	
death of a pet	50	
dealing with puberty	48	
problems in a romantic relationship	45	
fired from a job	40	
use of drugs or alcohol	40	
increase in fighting with parent(s) or sibling(s)	38	
confusion about sexual identity	35	
started a new job	30	
working while attending school	30	
increase in extracurricular activities	28	
major purchase (e.g., car)	25	
outstanding personal achievement	25	
began a new romantic relationship	20	
lack of privacy	15	
began or ended school year	10	

TOTAL SCORE _____   *Note—People who score higher than 250 may be overstressed and may develop a stress-related illness

What Is Their Life Change Index?

Using the previous worksheet, The Life Change Index, calculate the index for the following people.

1. Miroslav recently broke up with his girlfriend. He lives at home, where he shares a bedroom with his twin brother. He just started college this past fall. Fortunately, the college is in his hometown, so he didn't have to move.

   Life change index: _____

2. Wu proposed to his girlfriend because he got her pregnant. The baby is due in four months, and Wu just got a new job to help support his new family. At the moment, he's trying to juggle work and school. Wu hopes the new baby will be a girl because he wants to name it after his grandmother, who passed away two months ago.

   Life change index: _____

3. Ever since Alison's parents announced three months ago that they were separating, Alison's grades have slipped in school. She's so depressed about her home situation that she even slept through a few shifts at work and got fired from her part-time job.

   Life change index: _____

4. Loretta's cat died last month, which caused Loretta to feel depressed. Her depression was heightened last week when she and her boyfriend got into a major fight, and when she learned that her grandfather has been diagnosed with terminal cancer.

   Life change index: _____

5. Eytan's parents won the lottery a few months ago. With their winnings, his parents decided to move the family from their home in Iowa to a new mansion in Florida. Eytan misses his friends in Iowa and is having trouble fitting into his new school.

   Life change index: _____

6. Jackson's life has been going amazingly well this past year, so he's not sure why he's feeling so stressed. He just bought a new motorcycle with the money he saved from his part-time job. He's held this job for the past two years and works in the evenings after school. He also just won a spot on the National Junior Hockey Team, which means he's practicing hockey 12 hours a week instead of 6 hours a week.

   Life change index: _____

Choose one of these six people and offer some tips that will help this person cope with the stress in his or her life.

Good Stress versus Bad Stress

Stress can be positive or negative. What may be bad stress for one person can be good stress for another, and vice versa. It is also important to note that even good stress can cause negative reactions. For example, many married couples agree that while their wedding day was the most important day of their lives, it was also one of the most stressful.

For each of the following situations, write BAD in the blank space if you think you would find this situation negative, and write GOOD if you would find it positive.

_____ Moving to a new state and starting a new school

_____ Going out on a first date with someone you've liked for a long time

_____ Going away to camp for the summer to work as a counselor

_____ Presenting a seminar in front of your class

_____ Going to a party where you only know a few people

_____ Finding out that you (or your partner) is pregnant

_____ Meeting your boyfriend's/girlfriend's parents for the first time

_____ Performing in a play/sport/band in front of a crowd of thousands

_____ Looking after a baby for a day

_____ Going on a trip with your family to a country where you do not speak the language

_____ Having a teacher read aloud in class something you have written

_____ Traveling on your own to a large city that you have never visited before

Top 10 Sources of Stress

Here is a list of stress factors described in Diana Bohmer's article, "The Top 10 Sources of Stress for Kids." Put a check mark in the space on the left-hand side of the item if you can relate to it.

_____ Parent (or parents) having problems

_____ Having a fight with a friend or sibling

_____ Taking a test

_____ Wondering if someone thinks you're attractive (teens especially)

_____ Not having enough privacy

_____ Birth of a brother or sister

_____ Moving to a new school

_____ Remarriage (or marriage) of a parent

_____ Not having enough money

_____ Having a teacher who doesn't like you

Now create your own list of the 10 things that cause stress in your life.

1. _____

2. _____

3. _____

4. _____

5. _____

6. _____

7. _____

8. _____

9. _____

10. _____

NAME   DATE

Stress in Various Aspects of Your Life

People have different stresses in each aspect of their lives. For example, your stress with your family may be trying to convince your parents that you need a later curfew, while your stress with your friends might be in convincing them that you don't want to try smoking. Complete each circle by describing some of the stresses you have with whomever or whatever is mentioned in the center of the circle.

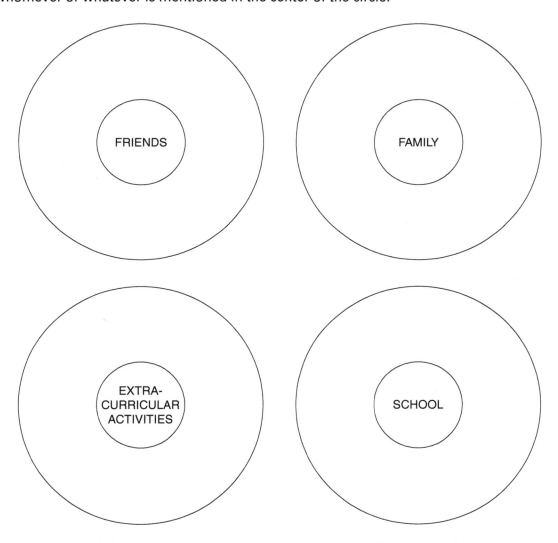

FRIENDS

FAMILY

EXTRA-CURRICULAR ACTIVITIES

SCHOOL

130

Three Generations of Stress

Stress is different for everyone, but it is particularly different for people of different age groups. For example, the stress you dealt with when you were three or four years old was probably quite different from the stress you feel in your life now. To examine the different stresses of different ages, compare your stress today with the stresses that your parents and grandparents are currently dealing with.

In the appropriate spaces, provide examples of things that are stressful in your life and then provide examples of things that your parents and grandparents find stressful. Then on another sheet of paper answer the questions that follow.

Your stresses: _____

_____

_____

_____

Your parents' stresses: _____

_____

_____

_____

Your grandparents' stresses: _____

_____

_____

_____

1. What observations can you make about the different stresses of the three generations?

2. How are your stresses different from those of your parents and grandparents?

3. How are your stresses similar to those of your parents and grandparents?

Long-Term Stress versus
Short-Term Stress

Long-term stress is caused by high levels of adrenaline over long periods of time. It might be triggered by something like dealing with the lengthy breakup of your parents' marriage or watching a parent slowly die of cancer. In contrast, short-term stress, such as performing in a play or a sports game, means you deal with high levels of adrenaline over a short period of time.

Complete the chart by describing five examples of both long-term and short-term stresses in your life.

LONG-TERM STRESS	SHORT-TERM STRESS
1.	1.
2.	2.
3.	3.
4.	4.
5.	5.

ZZZzzz: Sleep Patterns

One factor that can increase a person's stress level is sleep—or lack of it. If people don't get enough sleep, their tolerance levels and ability to deal with stress may decrease. Complete this survey by examining your sleep patterns in the last week to see if sleep is a problem affecting your stress level.

		Never	Rarely	Sometimes	Often	Always
1.	Do you get fewer than seven hours of sleep a night?	1	2	3	4	5
2.	Do you wake up during the night and have trouble getting back to sleep?	1	2	3	4	5
3.	Do you find that you are tired during the day and need to take a nap?	1	2	3	4	5
4.	Do you hit the snooze button on your alarm clock a few times and have difficulty getting out of bed in the morning?	1	2	3	4	5
5.	Do you have trouble falling asleep at night?	1	2	3	4	5
6.	Do you have nightmares or intense dreams?	1	2	3	4	5
7.	Does the temperature of your room cause you difficulty in sleeping?	1	2	3	4	5
8.	Do you have a pet who keeps you awake or wakes you up during the night?	1	2	3	4	5
9.	Do you hear noises inside or outside your house that keep you up?	1	2	3	4	5
10.	Do you share a bedroom with someone who snores or makes other noises?	1	2	3	4	5

If you scored 40 and above, your sleep patterns may affect your stress levels. You may want to reexamine your sleep patterns, so that you get a better night's sleep.

Sources-of-Stress Game

In each square, decipher which source of stress is being described. For example, becoming overweight is the source of stress described in Square A1.

	A	**B**	**C**	**D**
1	becoming weight	hope in the future	he art	famdeathily
2	feeling	getting knocked	BANKBALANCE	m o o d
3	worked paid	schstressool	A+ B- C D+ F	SAT scores
4	responsibility	fam ily	friends	resichangedence

NAME   DATE

The Four Stages of Stress

Below is a list of the four stages of stress and an explanation for each. A person may or may not go through all four stages of stress. Also note that the stressor is the incident that causes stress.

- **Stage 1: The alarm stage.** This stage occurs immediately after or during a stressful event. It includes the person's initial response to stress—for example, sweaty palms or a knot in the stomach.
- **Stage 2: The resistance stage.** Although the stressor continues, during this stage the person tries to act as normal as possible. The person may also try to escape from the stressor.
- **Stage 3: The adaptation stage.** The person has adapted to the stressor and continues to act normally in spite of the stress.
- **Stage 4: The exhaustion stage.** At this stage, the person can no longer pretend the stressor doesn't exist, and he or she becomes depressed, ill, or emotionally unstable.

Which stage is being described?

1. _____ After a boy's parents fight, the boy leaves the house and goes down the street to play with his friends.

2. _____ A boy's parents get into an argument and the boy's immediate reaction is to get upset.

3. _____ The boy's parents' fighting continues to the point where he can no longer ignore the fights. Fearing that his parents will get a divorce, the boy breaks down at school and cries while he explains the problem to his teacher.

4. _____ Although the boys' parents fight regularly, the boy acts as if there are no problems at home.

Fight or Flight

Some people react to stress by fighting, while others react by taking flight. Fighters are aggressive, whereas people who take flight try to avoid the stressful situation. Neither method is a healthy way of dealing with stress. For each situation listed below, write *flight* if the person is handling the stressful situation by running away, or write *fight* if the person's reaction is aggressive.

1. _____ Carla reacts to her parents' fights by going on a shoplifting spree.

2. _____ Alphina decides to avoid the stress of studying for exams by taking a three-hour nap.

3. _____ Yolanda's mother gives Yolanda an unrealistic curfew before a big party, so Yolanda yells at her mother.

4. _____ Some kids at school are picking on Jason, so he retreats to the school library during lunch and reads fantasy and science fiction books.

5. _____ Anh is not getting along with her boyfriend, so she escapes the situation by drinking alcohol and doing drugs.

6. _____ Abdi's parents are having marital problems, so rather than deal with the problems at home, Abdi spends extra hours at school playing basketball in the gym.

7. _____ Phil is failing at school. He's so angry with his marks that he smashes his fist into his locker.

8. _____ Four-year-old Jessica's mother passed away. Since her mother's death, Jessica has created an imaginary friend named Laura.

Those Stressful Reactions

Everyone reacts differently to stress. We have physical, emotional, and behavioral reactions. Following are some common physical, emotional, and behavioral reactions that people have to stress. Circle the reactions that you experience when you are stressed. At the end of each list are some spaces for you to write down some other examples that affect you but are not included on the list.

PHYSICAL	EMOTIONAL	BEHAVIORAL
acne	denial	over-talkative
grinding of teeth	fear	silent
sweaty palms	loss of emotional control	emotional outbursts
headaches	intense anger	loss of appetite
nausea	anxiety	increase of appetite
rapid heart beat	irritability	inability to sleep
vomiting	depression	pacing
dizziness	guilt	fear of being alone
sweaty armpits	agitation	desire to be alone
nail biting	inappropriate laughter	desire to sleep

Reacting to Stressful Situations

Sometimes harmless situations turn into stressful situations because of people's reactions. For example, imagine that an employee gives you the wrong order at a fast-food restaurant, and you react by yelling and screaming at the employee, his coworkers, and his manager. Suddenly you've turned an innocent mistake into a stressful situation. That innocent mistake could easily have been rectified by politely pointing out the problem to the employee.

Below are some situations. For each situation, write down a healthy reaction and an unhealthy reaction in the appropriate spots on the chart.

The Stressful Situation	A Healthy Reaction	An Unhealthy Reaction
A person in the cafeteria line trips, bumps into you, and causes you to fall forward into a tray of food. The food ruins your new, expensive shirt.		
You are an average student who spends weeks on an essay. The teacher gives your essay a failing grade and accuses you of plagiarism. You definitely did not plagiarize the paper.		
You find out that your boy/girlfriend lied to you about where he/she was last night. He/She was actually out at the movies with his old girl/boyfriend. He/She claims they are just friends.		
As you walk down the street on a rainy day, a car rushes past and drives through a huge puddle, spraying you from head to toe with muddy water.		

Relaxation Bingo

Find someone in your class who deals with stress by relaxing in one of the ways described in the following boxes. Ask the person to sign his or her name in the appropriate box. Try to find a different person for each of the 24 activities.

listens to music	keeps a diary or writes poetry	plays an instrument	takes a nap or sunbathes	goes for a walk or jog
goes out dancing	gets a massage	paints or enjoys making a craft	uses tools and builds something	does yoga
watches TV or a movie	sits in a hot tub, pool, or sauna	**FREE SPACE**	plays with a child or a pet	meditates
reads a book	finds a private place where no one can bother him or her	talks on the phone	gets together with a friend	does an active sport
rides a bike or drives a car	eats food	goes shopping	takes a bath or a shower	sings

Now put a check mark in the boxes that describe things YOU do to cope with stress.

NAME

Getting Physical

Sometimes the best way to deal with stress is by getting physical. Some people find punching a pillow releases frustration, while others just need a hug. Put a check mark beside the physical activity that helps you eliminate stress.

receive a hug	
dance	
jog	
in-line skate	
work out with weights	
hit something	
shoot baskets	
participate in a sport	
get a massage	
receive a back rub	
go for a walk	
ride a bike	
take an aerobics class	
drive	
meditate or do yoga	
pace	
other (specify below)	

Support Systems

Unfortunately, stress and upsetting situations are a part of life. No one is immune. In order to cope with stress, we obviously need coping mechanisms, but we also need a shoulder to cry on and people to talk to. It is important to have a support system of friends and family you can turn to in emergency situations.

Complete the following chart by writing in the names of 10 people in your support system. These people may be family members, friends, counselors, teachers, coaches, spiritual leaders, and so on. Include a phone number or other way of contacting the person.

Name of the Support Person	Relationship to You	Phone Number or Method of Contact

How Can You Help Your
Stressed Friend?

In the space after each case study, offer your suggestions for how to help your stressed friend.

Case Study I

Your friend, Brooke, is under considerable stress. Her parents are separating because her father is having an affair. Brooke is quite close to her dad and is really upset that he's moving out. Lately this "A" student's grades have dropped to the point where she is failing. Brooke has become moody and has been dumped by her boyfriend because of this moodiness. For years, Brooke has been rather thin, but lately she's lost so much weight that you think she might suffer from an eating disorder. *How can you help your stressed friend?*

_____

_____

_____

_____

_____

_____

Case Study II

Last year Carl's parents and brother were killed in a car crash caused by a drunk driver. Understandably, Carl has been depressed, but he doesn't seem able to move past this stage. Last month he dropped out of school, moved out of his aunt and uncle's house, and talked about joining his family in heaven. You are concerned that Carl is suicidal. *How can you help your friend?*

_____

_____

_____

_____

_____

A Suicide Awareness Quiz

For each of the following statements, circle TRUE if you think the statement is true and FALSE if you think the statement is false.

1. TRUE or FALSE: A person who unsuccessfully attempts suicide or thinks about suicide will have suicidal thoughts the rest of his or her life.

2. TRUE or FALSE: If a friend confides in you that he or she has been thinking about committing suicide and then asks you not to tell anyone, you must respect his or her wish for privacy.

3. TRUE or FALSE: Most people who attempt suicide don't actually want to die.

4. TRUE or FALSE: Poor people are more likely to commit suicide than rich people.

5. TRUE or FALSE: Many people who commit suicide never talk about it before doing it.

6. TRUE or FALSE: Suicide is usually genetic—that is, it tends to run in families.

7. TRUE or FALSE: If you discuss suicide with a friend you are concerned about, this may encourage him or her to commit suicide.

8. TRUE or FALSE: A person who plans to commit suicide cannot be helped or talked out of attempting suicide by anyone other than a professional psychiatrist.

9. TRUE or FALSE: All people who commit suicide have some sort of drug or alcohol addiction problem.

Dealing with a Grieving Friend

Imagine that your closest friend is dealing with the death of a parent or sibling. Below are some statements describing how people might support such a friend. If the support is appropriate, write DO in the space next to the statement. If the support might not be helpful or appropriate, write DON'T in the space next to the statement.

1. _____ Avoid the grieving friend and wait for him or her to contact you.

2. _____ Tell the friend that this was "God's will" or "It was the person's time."

3. _____ Help the friend by offering to run errands, to bring food, and to help with homework.

4. _____ Talk about memories you have of the deceased.

5. _____ Ask the friend what you can do to help.

6. _____ Be with the grieving friend constantly and avoid giving him or her time alone.

7. _____ Try to persuade the friend to stop crying and encourage him or her to deal with things and move on quickly.

8. _____ Listen and allow the grieving friend to talk, cry, share, and discuss his or her feelings.

9. _____ Act like a psychologist and explain why the grieving friend is acting the way he or she is.

10. _____ Let the friend laugh or cry. Recognize that both emotions are healthy.

Thoughts on Death and Dying

Answer each of the following questions with your honest opinion and response.

1. What do you think will happen to you after you die? _____
_____
_____

2. Do you believe in ghosts? Explain. _____
_____
_____

3. If you were brain-dead and in a coma, do you think your family would have the right to ask that the plug be pulled? Would you want the plug pulled, or would you prefer to remain in a coma? _____
_____
_____

4. If you were close to death, would you want your organs donated to someone who needed a transplant? Explain your answer. _____
_____
_____

5. Do you think euthanasia should be a legal option for people with a terminal illness?
_____
_____
_____

6. Do you believe that people have guardian angels? Do you believe in angels?
_____
_____
_____

The Five Stages of Grief

When people lose someone close to them or learn that they are dying, they go through five stages of grief. (These phases were researched and described by Dr. Elisabeth Kubler-Ross.) People do not necessarily go through all of the stages or go through the stages in order. Unfortunately, some people never reach the fifth stage. The five stages are listed here along with a brief description of each one.

Imagine that someone you know is dealing with the loss of a parent or family member. In the spaces, provide an example of something this person might say or do while in that stage of grieving.

Stage 1: Denial and isolation. At this stage people tend to isolate themselves from family and friends. Also, in the shock of the situation, they tend to deny the loss has taken place.

_____

_____

Stage 2: Anger. People express anger at God, themselves, the victim, or others.

_____

_____

Stage 3: Bargaining. People make bargains (often with God) that they will do something or give something if God makes the victim well again.

_____

_____

Stage 4: Depression. People have accepted that the person has died, and now they go into depression as they mourn the loss.

_____

_____

Stage 5: Acceptance. Although the grieving person will never be happy about the loss, at this stage, the death has been accepted and the person is able to move forward to a new life without the deceased person.

_____

_____

NAME _____ DATE

Which Stage of Grief
(in Dying Patients)?

Read each scenario and determine which stage of grief, according to Kubler-Ross's theory, each person is in. Write this stage in the space provided.

1. Denise, who has cancer, found herself yelling and screaming in her kitchen. She threw pots and pans around as she did the dishes. Her doctor provoked her temper tantrum when he told her earlier in the day that this would probably be her last Christmas.

   Stage of grief: _____

2. Marek, another cancer victim, is celebrating his life by writing letters to all of his friends. He just took his final trip to his cottage in the country, and is enjoying his final days by smelling the roses and making the most of each day.

   Stage of grief: _____

3. Bryan, who is dying, has begged God to let him live long enough to see his daughter get married.

   Stage of grief: _____

4. Ken just found out that his ex-lover tested positive for HIV. Ken has experienced some of the symptoms of AIDS, but he refuses to get tested. He's terrified of the truth. Ken has also avoided seeing many of his friends in the gay community since finding out about his ex-lover's illness.

   Stage of grief: _____

5. Since Jessica is dying, she has decided not to put up the Christmas tree this year. She figures why bother since she could be dead before Christmas. She also spends most of her days crying.

   Stage of grief: _____

FOOD AND FOOD-RELATED ISSUES

We live in an age when pizza gets to
your house before the police.

Jeff Marder

NAME _____ DATE

Food Associations

Food is not only physically nourishing but also emotionally satisfying. We often associate certain food items with specific occasions or experiences. For example, a slice of chocolate cake may remind you of your birthday. In the space provided on the chart below, list the first food that comes to mind for each situation or phrase.

The Situation	The Food You Associate With This Situation
a hot day	
a cold day	
a family holiday	
your birthday	
sick with a cold	
feeling sad	
feeling stressed	
staying up late to do homework	
a childhood memory	
love	
out with your friends	
on the go and in a rush	
a celebration	
a sporting event	
at the movies	
on a picnic	

A Healthy-Eating Report Card

Think about what you have eaten in the last week. Answer the questions by putting a check mark in the appropriate column.

	Excellent	Average	Needs Improvement
How many servings from the bread, cereal, rice, and pasta food group do you eat each day?	6-11 servings	3-5 servings	0-2 servings
How many servings from the vegetable food group do you eat each day?	3-5 servings	1-2 servings	0 serving
How many servings from the fruit food group do you eat each day?	2-4 servings	1 serving	0 serving
How many servings from the meat, poultry, fish, eggs, and nuts group do you eat each day?	2-3 servings	1 serving	0 serving or 4+ servings
How many servings from the milk, yogurt, and cheese group do you eat each day?	2-3 servings	1 serving	0 serving or 4+ servings
Do you eat healthy snacks instead of unhealthy snacks?	Always	Sometimes	Never

If you are not sure what is considered a serving, the following information may help.

A serving is a slice of bread; a piece of fruit; a half-cup of cooked pasta; two ounces of processed cheese; two to three ounces of cooked lean meat, poultry, or fish; one egg; two tablespoons of peanut butter; one cup of raw leafy vegetables; a half-cup of cooked vegetables; one cup of milk; and three-quarters of a cup of fruit juice. Remember too that just because you eat one plate of spaghetti, for example, does not mean that it is one serving. It may count as two or three servings.

Comment on the areas on which you need to improve. How do you plan to improve your eating habits in these areas?

_____

_____

_____

_____

_____

_____

NAME DATE

An Eating-Habits Survey

Complete this survey by answering each question as honestly as you can.

1. Who buys most of the food at your house? _____

2. Who prepares most of the meals at your house? _____

3. How many meals a day do you eat? _____

4. If you skip meals, which meal or meals do you skip the most often? _____
    _____

5. How often in a month do you eat at a fast-food restaurant? _____

6. How often in a month do you eat at a regular restaurant? _____

7. How often in a day do you snack? _____

8. What time of day do you usually snack? _____

9. Do you sometimes eat when you're not hungry? _____

10. What type of food do you avoid eating? _____

11. What food do you crave the most? _____

12. How much water do you drink in a day? _____

13. Does your family usually enjoy a meal together, or do you often eat separately?
    _____

14. Where do you eat most of your meals (for example, in front of the TV, at the table,
    and so on)? _____

15. Do you take vitamins or supplements? _____

15a. If so, which ones? _____

16. If you eat when you're studying, what do you eat? _____

17. If you eat when you're stressed, what do you eat? _____

18. Do you eat when you watch TV or a movie? _____

After you have completed this survey, trade with a classmate. On a separate piece of paper list the concerns you have about that person's eating habits. When you get your paper back with your classmate's comments, write your own evaluation of your eating habits. Do you agree or disagree with the comments made by your classmate?

Favorite Food

One benefit of living in America is the variety of food we can find here. Fresh produce is grown from one coast to the other. Companies like Hershey and Heinz satisfy all different types of tastebuds with the incredible variety of foods they produce. As a multicultural country, America also imports foods from all over the world.

Imagine that you have won a contest where a chef will provide your favorite meals. Use this sheet to design your ideal menu for a day.

BREAKFAST

LUNCH

DINNER

After studying your menu, answer the following questions:

1. Is this menu balanced? _____

2. Which food groups tend to dominate the menu? _____

    _____

3. What does the menu reveal about you? _____

    _____

    _____

    _____

NAME _____ DATE _____

A Food Pyramid Puzzle

The USDA's Food Pyramid Guide outlines what Americans should eat each day. Complete the empty pyramid by indicating the number of recommended servings for each food group.

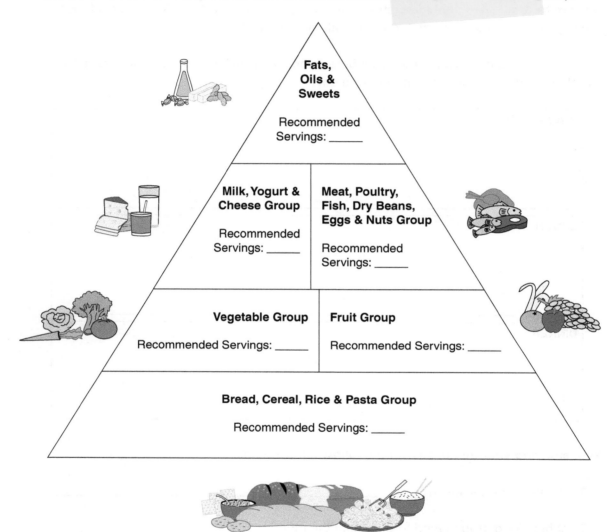

Fats, Oils & Sweets

Recommended Servings: _____

Milk, Yogurt & Cheese Group

Recommended Servings: _____

Meat, Poultry, Fish, Dry Beans, Eggs & Nuts Group

Recommended Servings: _____

Vegetable Group

Recommended Servings: _____

Fruit Group

Recommended Servings: _____

Bread, Cereal, Rice & Pasta Group

Recommended Servings: _____

NAME DATE

Factors Affecting Your Food Choices

A number of factors affect what we choose to eat. For each factor listed below, provide examples of how this factor affects your food choices and eating habits.

1. **Family:** What your family eats determines what you will eat. For instance, if your mom or dad dislikes seafood, then you probably won't eat much seafood.

    Describe how *your* family affects *your* food choices._____

    _____

2. **Culture:** The American population consists of many different cultures. Your cultural background probably determines the types of food that you eat, along with your other eating habits.

    Describe how *your* culture affects *your* food choices._____

    _____

3. **Peers:** Like your family, your friends can also have a significant impact on the types of food you eat. For example, if your friends go to McDonald's for lunch every day, this will probably influence your eating habits.

    Describe how *your* friends affect *your* food choices._____

    _____

4. **Media:** The media plays a significant role in our lives. If your favorite characters on a TV show drink a certain type of soda, then studies show you will probably drink that soda too. Also, TV commercials and other kinds of ads persuade us to eat certain foods.

    Describe how the media affects *your* food choices. _____

    _____

5. **Personal health and allergies:** People are more aware than ever before of food allergies. Also, people often have health concerns that affect their food choices.

    Describe how *your* health and allergies affect *your* food choices._____

    _____

NAME   DATE

"Weight" and See

The rate of obesity among Americans is increasing rapidly to the point where more than half the population is now overweight. Six factors influence our weight: behavior, health, genetics, environment, culture, and income level. In the chart below, suggest how these factors affect *your* weight.

The Six Factors That Influence Our Weight	Ways in Which These Six Factors Affect *Your* Weight
BEHAVIOR	
HEALTH STATUS	
GENETICS	
ENVIRONMENT	
CULTURE	
INCOME LEVEL	

A Day in the Life of Your Stomach

Recall everything that you ate and drank yesterday. Absolutely everything! In the chart below, list everything you consumed from the moment you woke up to the moment you went to sleep. Then, in Column A, put a check mark beside the items that have nutritional value. In Column B, put a check mark beside the items that you did not need to consume or that have no nutritional value. Which column has more check marks? What does this exercise reveal about your eating habits?

	A	B		A	B

NAME   DATE

Calorie Calculations

A calorie is the unit used to measure the energy that a food yields in the body. If your body consumes more calories than it needs, the extra "energy" will be stored as fat. One pound of fat equals 3,500 calories.

How many calories do you need? According to Margo Fienden, whose book *The Calorie Factor* is the basis for many of these statistics, "The desirable weight for a [person] is the weight at which [he or she] feels comfortable. Period."

Here is a list of the calories in some selected foods:

Fruit (Calories)

- One cup of strawberries (53)
- One grapefruit (84)
- One apple (80)
- One orange (56)
- One banana (81)

Dessert (Calories)

- One piece of blueberry pie (382)
- One piece of chocolate cake (without icing) (206)
- One piece of gum (10)
- One sandwich cookie with cream filling (50)
- One oatmeal cookie (24)
- Ten potato chips (113)
- One pretzel (4)
- One ice cream bar (180)

Veggies (Calories)

- One serving of cooked broccoli (20)
- One serving of cooked cabbage (17)
- Half-cup of carrots (22)
- One tomato (raw) (27)

Dinner and Meat (Calories)

- One slice of bacon (73)
- One egg (cooked) (80)
- One serving of pork and beans (130)
- One serving of beef stew (209)
- One piece of cooked chicken (87)
- One package of macaroni and cheese (203)
- One slice of cheese pizza (267)
- One spaghetti dinner with meat (251)

Beverages (Calories)

- Half-cup of apple juice (58)
- One bottle of beer (145)
- One glass of cola (97)
- One glass of milk (81)
- One milkshake (small) (259)

Others (Calories)

- One teaspoon of margarine (34)
- One teaspoon of butter (34)
- One tablespoon of peanut butter (100)
- One piece of white bread (64)
- One serving of cottage cheese (105)
- One muffin (bran) (125)

How many calories are in these meals?

Meal 1

One glass of milk

Two pieces of bread with peanut butter (one tablespoon)

One banana

Total _____

Meal 2

One bottle of beer

One spaghetti dinner with meat

One dish of strawberries

One piece of blueberry pie

Total _____

Meal 3

Two slices of pizza

One milkshake (small)

One bag of chips (50 chips per bag)

Total _____

Meal 4

Three slices of bacon

Two cooked eggs

One muffin with a teaspoon of butter

One glass of apple juice (one cup)

Total _____

Using this calorie list as a guide, see if you can calculate approximately how many calories you consume in an average day.

NAME _____   DATE _____

What to Know About H$_2$O

Here are some statements about water. Unfortunately, the statements are all missing some important information. Fill in the blanks by putting the correct words and numbers from the following list in the correct spaces.

two to three quarts	juice	two-thirds
nutrient	six to eight	caffeine
water	dehydrated	

1. Water is the most important _____ and is essential for life.

2. Your body is _____ water.

3. We can survive for days without fats, carbohydrates, protein, vitamins, and minerals, but we can't survive more than a few days without _____.

4. Each day, we lose _____ of water through feces, urine, sweat, and breathing.

5. If you are thirsty, that's a sign that you are_____ and need to drink water.

6. Along with a glass of water, you can get your water intake from milk, soup, and

   _____.

7. Do not count fluids that contain _____ as part of your water intake because of their diuretic (water-loss) effect.

8. You should drink _____ glasses of water each day.

NAME DATE

Let's Learn About Vitamins

Vitamins do not provide calories, but they are essential in helping the body make use of the calories it consumes. There are various types of vitamins, and for each type there are specific foods that provide us with these vitamins.

Here is a list of some of the vitamins we need and why we need them. Following each one is a multiple-choice list of four foods. Only one food in each group is a good source of the vitamin listed. Circle the letter next to the food that belongs to the vitamin.

1. **Vitamin A**—needed for tooth enamel, calcium, and bone formation.
   a. Fish
   b. Sunlight
   c. Milk
   d. Oranges

2. **Vitamin B1**—(thiamin)-changes glucose into fat or energy and maintains our appetite.
   a. Whole-grain cereals
   b. Eggs
   c. Spinach
   d. Tomatoes

3. **Vitamin B2**—(riboflavin)-transports hydrogen and keeps the skin healthy.
   a. Sugar
   b. Orange juice
   c. Lettuce
   d. Onions

4. **Vitamin C (ascorbic acid)**—helps heal wounds and boosts the immune system.
   a. Milk
   b. Oranges
   c. Yeast
   d. Cheese

5. **Vitamin D**—helps with tooth and bone development.
   a. Cabbage
   b. Orange juice
   c. Fish
   d. Wheat germ

6. **Vitamin E**—helps protect us from red blood cell destruction.
   a. Grapefruit
   b. Lettuce
   c. Sunlight
   d. Wheat germ

NAME _____   DATE _____

Cholesterol: Fact or Fiction

Read each of the following statements and decide whether the information is true or false. If the information is true, circle the word FACT. If it is false, circle the word FICTION.

1. FACT or FICTION: Cholesterol is important for cell development, the formation of sex hormones, and the formation of the digestive juices, and it is an important component of the membranes that hold cells together.

2. FACT or FICTION: Cholesterol is the same thing as fat.

3. FACT or FICTION: We actually don't need to eat cholesterol because our bodies are capable of producing all the cholesterol we need.

4. FACT or FICTION: Cholesterol travels to and from the liver to cells by way of the bloodstream. Since it cannot move in the bloodstream on its own, it is carried by lipoproteins.

5. FACT or FICTION: Lipoproteins are produced in the small intestine.

6. FACT or FICTION: Low-density lipoproteins (LDL) are considered good because these carriers of cholesterol carefully remove cholesterol from the cells, carrying it all the way back to the liver.

7. FACT or FICTION: High-density lipoproteins (HDL) are considered bad because they are more likely to "stick" to blood vessel walls, and this can eventually contribute to heart attacks or strokes.

8. FACT or FICTION: When you get a blood test, it is important to have a greater amount of high-density lipoproteins than low-density lipoproteins.

9. FACT or FICTION: Every food coming from animals—like eggs, cheese, meat, fish, and poultry—contains cholesterol.

10. FACT or FICTION: Cholesterol is not found in plant oils or plant foods.

Protein Fill-in-the-Blanks

Use the words in the following list to complete the blanks in this paragraph about protein.

cheese	amino acids	oxygen	tissues
growth	manufacture	animal	protein
cell	rice	nuts	22
nine	energy	biological	10 to 12

People need protein for many reasons. For example, protein is a source of

_____. It is necessary for _____ and the repair of

_____. Protein also helps transport _____ and nutrients

throughout the body. Protein is needed for every _____ of our body,

and it is made up of _____. There are _____ different

amino acids, and the various types found in protein determine its _____

activity. Our bodies _____ 13 of the amino acids, but not the other

_____ . Since we need those nine amino acids in order to function,

_____ is very important in our diets. Many _____

products are good sources of protein; for example, poultry, eggs, milk, fish, meat,

and _____. Other sources of protein are peanut butter, _____ ,

beans, seeds, _____ , and grains. People need to get _____

percent of their calories from protein.

NAME _____   DATE

All You Ever Wanted to Know About Fiber

Fiber comes from the part of a plant that human enzymes cannot digest. Since we don't digest fiber, we get no calories or energy from it. So why is fiber important? It helps regulate our bowels, prevents constipation, and lowers our blood cholesterol levels. There are two main types of fiber: soluble fiber, which dissolves in water, and insoluble fiber, which does not dissolve in water.

Put a check mark in the blank space next to the foods that provide us with fiber.

____ Bran cereals	____ Carrots
____ Milk	____ Sandwich cookies with cream filling
____ Whole-grain bread	____ Figs
____ Popcorn	____ White potatoes
____ Steak	____ Peanut butter
____ Apples	____ Oranges
____ Jellybeans	____ Chocolate
____ Strawberries	____ Oatmeal
____ Cheese	____ Turnips
____ Corn	____ Yogurt

NAME _____   DATE

Fat Habits and You

Circle yes or no to the following questions.

1. YES or NO: Do you usually eat French fries with your meals when you eat out?

2. YES or NO: Do you drink homogenized milk?

3. YES or NO: Do you eat a doughnut, muffin, or pastry for most breakfasts?

4. YES or NO: Do you fry most of your food (rather than roast, boil, or steam)?

5. YES or NO: Do you put butter or sour cream (or both) on vegetables or baked potatoes?

6. YES or NO: Do you put butter on toast, hot dog buns, or hamburger buns?

7. YES or NO: Do you eat hot dogs, luncheon meat, or sausages more than twice a week?

8. YES or NO: Do you regularly snack on chips or cookies?

9. YES or NO: Do you put mayonnaise on hamburgers and sandwiches?

10. YES or NO: Do you put lots of salad dressing on your salads?

11. YES or NO: Do you eat chicken with the skin or fried chicken?

12. YES or NO: Do you eat bacon more than once a week?

The more yes answers you have, the higher your fat intake. Examine your answers, and in the space provided, determine what you can do to change your fat habits.

_____

_____

_____

_____

_____

Fat Classification

There are three classifications of fat: monounsaturated fat, polyunsaturated fat, and saturated fat. Foods often consist of a combination of different fats. For example, peanut butter is 48 percent monounsaturated fat, 33 percent polyunsaturated fat, and 19 percent saturated fat.

Below is a description of each of these three fat classifications. Following this is a chart of food. If the food mentioned is mainly a source of monounsaturated fats, write an M in the blank column to the right of the food. If the food is mainly a source of polyunsaturated fats, write P in the blank column, and if the food is mainly a source of saturated fats, write an S in the blank column.

- **Monounsaturated fats:** Along with polyunsaturated fats, monounsaturated fats are considered healthier for people than saturated fats. Monounsaturated fats generally come from foods that come from plants, nuts, and seeds. They can lower LDL cholesterol (bad cholesterol) without decreasing HDL cholesterol (good cholesterol).

- **Polyunsaturated fats:** These fats usually are liquid at room temperature. They are good because they tend to lower blood cholesterol levels. This type of fat is found in nuts, vegetable oils, and fatty fish.

- **Saturated fats:** These fats are considered bad because they raise blood cholesterol. Unlike polyunsaturated fats, they are generally solid at room temperature. Sources of saturated fats include coconut and palm oils and fats from animal products.

BUTTER		OLIVES	
SUNFLOWER SEEDS		CREAM	
CHOCOLATE CAKE		WALNUTS	
POTATO CHIPS		CHEESE	
CANOLA OIL		PEANUT OIL	
FRENCH FRIES		SOYBEAN OIL	

Fat Reduction

Your body needs some fat in your daily diet. However, Americans often consume too much fat. The object of this exercise is to help you learn ways to reduce your fat intake. Compare the items in Columns A and B. Determine which one has fewer grams of fat. If the item in Column A is lower in fat, then put a check mark in the blank column at the left of Column A. If the item in Column B is lower in fat, then put a check mark in the blank column at the left of Column B.

	COLUMN A		COLUMN B
	1 glass of homogenized milk		1 glass of skim milk
	1/4 cup of grated cheddar cheese		1/4 cup of grated mozzarella cheese
	4 oz. chicken with no skin		4 oz. chicken with skin
	a ham sandwich with mustard		a ham sandwich with mayonnaise
	1/2 cup of unbuttered popcorn		1/2 cup peanuts
	1 avocado		1 pear
	1 bran muffin		1 croissant
	1 slice of apple pie		1 piece of apple crisp
	1/4 cup of cream cheese		1/4 cup of creamed cottage cheese
	1 boiled or poached egg		1 fried egg
	1 hamburger		1 tuna sandwich

Crazy About Carbohydrates

Loretta loves carbohydrates so much that she plans to write an article on this nutrient for her local newspaper. Below is a list of her research notes. If you think the information is correct, put a check mark in the YES column. If it is incorrect, put a check mark in the NO column and then rewrite the fact on the back of this sheet to make it correct.

	YES	NO
1. Carbohydrates are one of three main nutrients essential to living organisms. (The other two are protein and fats.)		
2. Carbohydrates' main job is to produce energy for the body.		
3. Chemically, carbohydrates are made up of carbon, hydrogen, and helium.		
4. The more inactive a person, the more carbohydrates he/she needs in his/her diet.		
5. There are two different forms of carbohydrates: simple and complex.		
6. Simple carbohydrates are one, two, or at the most three units of sugar linked together in a single molecule.		
7. Complex carbohydrates are hundreds or thousands of sugar units linked together in single molecules.		
8. Complex carbohydrates are found in sugars.		
9. Simple carbohydrates are found in grains, beans, fruits, vegetables, bread, pasta, cereal, and rice.		
10. Fats that are not used will be converted into carbohydrates.		
11. Without carbohydrates, the body cannot use the other two main ingredients —protein and fat—properly.		

NAME DATE

Our Addiction to Additives

Food additives are substances added to food either intentionally or accidentally. For instance, salt added to soup is an intentional additive. Meanwhile, a chemical sprayed on a plant that's used to control insects may remain on the plant. This is an example of an accidental additive. Here are some interesting facts about additives from *A Quick Guide to Food Safety* by Robert Goodman:

- Over 3,000 different chemicals are used (intentionally) in processed foods.

- The average American consumes approximately 150 pounds of additives per year.

- The most popular additives in America are sugar and salt.

Additives benefit both us—the people consuming food—and the industry—the people growing, making, and selling food. However, additives also have negative aspects. Complete this chart by listing as many advantages and disadvantages as you can think of for the use of additives in food.

ADVANTAGES	DISADVANTAGES

NAME DATE

Food Categories

Each nutrient listed below is followed by a series of boxes. In each box, write a food that supplies a person with this nutrient.

CARBOHYDRATES

PROTEIN

FIBER

POLYUNSATURATED FATS

NAME   DATE

Just Because It's a Salad Doesn't Mean It's Healthy

Many people automatically assume that salads are healthier than fast food. However, many salads include dressings and other ingredients that make them high in fat. Examine the following three salad recipes. For each salad, determine what makes it unhealthy and also what can be done to make the recipe healthier.

Caesar Salad

Romaine lettuce   Dressing: half-cup of Golden Caesar
Bacon bits   salad dressing, half-cup of
Croutons   mayonnaise, garlic

Directions: Place all the ingredients in bowl and toss with dressing.

What makes this salad unhealthy? _____

_____

What changes to the recipe could help make the salad healthier? _____

_____

Broccoli Salad

One bunch of broccoli, cut into florets   Four green onions, chopped fine
Half-pound of bacon, cooked,   Dressing: one cup of mayonnaise,
   drained, and crumbled   quarter-cup of sugar, two tablespoons
One cup of shredded cheddar cheese   of vinegar

Directions: Place all the ingredients in bowl and toss with dressing.

What makes this salad unhealthy? _____

_____

What changes to the recipe could help make the salad healthier? _____

_____

Five-Cup Salad

One cup of sour cream   One cup of mandarin oranges
One cup of shredded coconut   One cup of pineapple tidbits
One cup of miniature marshmallows

Directions: Mix ingredients ahead of time and chill.

What makes this salad unhealthy? _____

_____

What changes to the recipe could help make the salad healthier? _____

_____

Can You Help These Eaters?

Below are the daily diets of three different individuals. Make comments and suggestions on how these people can improve their daily diets.

Person 1

Breakfast: Coffee with cream and sugar, three fried eggs, four slices of bacon, two pieces of toast with butter and jam

Snack: Chocolate-covered doughnut and a coffee with cream and sugar

Lunch: Ham sandwich, French fries, soda, slice of pecan pie

Dinner: 10-ounce steak, baked potato with butter and sour cream, two ears of corn with butter, two bottles of beer, a dish of chocolate ice cream, and a slice of chocolate cake

Comments and suggestions: _____

_____

_____

Person 2

Breakfast: A glass of water

Lunch: A low-fat breakfast bar

Snack: A glass of water

Dinner: A plate of spaghetti with no sauce, a glass of water, and a peach

Comments and suggestions: _____

_____

_____

Person 3

Breakfast: A blueberry muffin, tea with milk

Snack: A glass of lemonade

Lunch: A peanut butter and jam sandwich on white bread, four cookies, a glass of homogenized milk, and an apple

Snack: A chocolate bar

Dinner: Three pieces of fried chicken, French fries, two glasses of soda, two chocolate brownies

Comments and suggestions: _____

_____

_____

An Eating Disorder True-False Quiz

According to the BodyWise Web site: "Eating disorders are extreme expressions of food and weight issues experienced by many individuals." Learn more about eating disorders by doing this true or false quiz. For each statement, circle TRUE if you believe the statement is true and FALSE if you believe the statement is false.

1. TRUE or FALSE: Almost 5 percent of young women in the United States are affected by eating disorders and as many as 15 percent of young women have unhealthy attitudes about food.

2. TRUE or FALSE: Boys and men do not develop eating disorders.

3. TRUE or FALSE: Anorexics eat large amounts of food and then take laxatives or induce vomiting to get rid of the food.

4. TRUE or FALSE: Bulimics have strange eating habits and often avoid eating food altogether.

5. TRUE or FALSE: Overeating or eating large amounts of food even when not hungry is considered an eating disorder.

6. TRUE or FALSE: If an eating disorder gets out of hand, it can be life-threatening.

7. TRUE or FALSE: Many people who suffer from eating disorders are depressed and feel a lack of control over their lives.

8. TRUE or FALSE: People only develop eating disorders in their midteens.

9. TRUE or FALSE: Research suggests that 1 percent of teenage girls suffer from anorexia nervosa.

Name That Disorder

Read the three scenarios below and decide whether the person suffers from compulsive eating, anorexia, or bulimia.

Scenario I

At age 13, Debbie was on her way to becoming a first-rate gymnast. She was always short for her age, but she had to fight to keep thin. One day a judge told Debbie that if she wanted to improve her tumbling, "she should lose some of that baby fat." Debbie took the comment seriously and began a strict diet. She stopped eating fast food and any fat, and she began to weigh her food and count her calories. A few months later, she stopped eating almost completely and survived on an apple and three pieces of toast a day. Debbie also exercised constantly. Even in bed, she'd wake up to do sit-ups. Debbie started wearing more and more clothes because she could never get warm enough.

What eating disorder does Debbie suffer from? _____

On a separate piece of paper make some suggestions for how Debbie could overcome this disorder.

Scenario II

Like all teenagers, Kesha wanted to fit in and look attractive to boys. She had tried to diet, but every diet failed. She was angry at herself for not dieting, so she ate everything in sight. Then she'd go to the bathroom and vomit. Kesha hid food in her room and would eat it at night when the family had gone to bed. She always vomited afterward. She also took laxatives regularly.

What eating disorder does Kesha suffer from? _____

On a separate piece of paper make some suggestions for how Kesha could overcome this disorder.

Scenario III

Ninth grade was a difficult year for Eduardo. His parents had recently separated, he did not make the football team, and his grades were suffering. Eduardo dealt with the situation by eating. He ate large amounts of food in one sitting and often ate until he felt uncomfortably full. Nevertheless, he ate normal amounts of food in front of family and friends, which caused people to wonder why he was gaining so much weight. However, in the privacy of his bedroom, he would binge on junk food and fast food.

What eating disorder does Eduardo suffer from? _____

On a separate piece of paper make some suggestions for how Eduardo could overcome this disorder.

Signs of an Eating Disorder

Listed below are some questions. Answer these questions yes or no. If you answer yes to at least half of the questions, then you may be at risk of developing an eating disorder. If you fall into this category, you may wish to seek professional help or discuss your eating habits with an adult you trust, like a school counselor.

1. YES or NO: Do you have an intense fear of becoming fat or gaining weight?

2. YES or NO: Do you weigh yourself at least once a day?

3. YES or NO: Do you have an obsession with knowing the amount of calories or grams of fat in the food you consume?

4. YES or NO: Do you prefer to eat alone?

5. YES or NO: Do you take laxatives or diuretics to help control your weight?

6. YES or NO: Do you exercise intensely for long periods of time with the intention of losing weight?

7. YES or NO: Are you a perfectionist or high achiever?

8. YES or NO: Do you sometimes induce vomiting after consuming a large amount of food?

9. YES or NO: Do you ever eat large amounts of food privately and avoid eating meals with your family?

10. YES or NO: If you are female, do you no longer get your period?

The Dos and Don'ts of Helping
Someone with an Eating Disorder

Unfortunately, an increasing number of women and men each year struggle with eating disorders. Naturally, friends and family members want to help, but sometimes the attempts to help can cause more problems.

Below is a list of things people sometimes do in order to help someone with an eating disorder. Write DO if you think the strategy would be helpful, or DON'T if you think it would not be helpful.

1. Force the person to eat or stop exercising. _____

2. Help the person find a professional who can help him or her to deal with

   the issues. _____

3. Blame yourself for the other person's problems. _____

4. Recognize that other, nonfood factors are part of the problem and try to help

   the person deal with those factors. _____

5. Avoid talking about the issue and hope the person will deal with the problem on his

   or her own. _____

6. Once the person gets professional help, tell him or her that you expect an instant

   recovery. _____

7. Avoid dwelling on food-related issues. _____

8. Avoid commenting on the person's weight and appearance even if these comments

   have positive intentions. _____

9. Learn as much as you can about the person's eating disorder and share what you

   learn with the person. _____

10. Encourage the person to get involved in nonfood-related activities. _____

NAME   DATE

The Food-Vocabulary Word Game

The left-hand side of the numbered list below presents definitions for food vocabulary. Read the definition and then write the term described in the spaces provided. (There is one space for each letter.) Last, write the circled letter in the appropriate space at the bottom of the page. For instance, the letter from definition 1 goes in the space above the number 1. These letters will create a message about eating. Note that some letters may be used more than once.

Here's a list of words from which to choose.

anorexia	sugar	starch	nutritionist	nutrient
water	fats	bulimia	minerals	caffeine
protein	monounsatur-	vegetarian	vitamin	calorie
carbohydrate	ated fat	calcium		

1. Any chemical substance found in food that is used by the body to survive. _ _ _ _ _ Ⓔ _ _

2. A mineral that builds bones and teeth. _Ⓒ_ _ _ _ _ _

3. A person who gives advice about healthy eating. _ _ Ⓣ _ _ _ _ _ _ _

4. The nutrient that's the body's most important source of energy. _ _ _ _ _ _ Ⓗ _ _ _ _ _

5. A sweet substance. Ⓢ_ _ _ _ _

6. A person who does not eat meat. _Ⓥ_ _ _ _ _ _ _ _

7. An eating disorder that involves self-induced vomiting. Ⓑ_ _ _ _ _ _

8. The unit for measuring the amount of energy that food supplies in the body. _ _Ⓛ_ _ _ _

9. An eating disorder that involves starvation. _Ⓝ_ _ _ _ _ _

10. A substance found in coffee and tea that stimulates the heart. Ⓒ_ _ _ _ _ _ _

11. A type of fat that lowers bad cholesterol and increases good cholesterol (2 words).
_ _ _ _ _ _ _ _ _ _ _ _ Ⓐ _ _ _ _

12. Inorganic elements that the body can't manufacture. Ⓜ_ _ _ _ _ _ _

13. A nutrient found in milk products, eggs, meat, poultry, and fish. _Ⓟ_ _ _ _ _ _

14. Provides energy & cushions and protects organs. _Ⓐ_ _

15. A white food substance found in most plants like potatoes and beans. _ _ _ _ _ Ⓗ

16. Organic chemicals that the body needs for metabolism. _ _ _Ⓘ_ _ _

17. The most essential nutrient. _Ⓦ_ _ _

MESSAGE:

___ ___ ___   ___ ___ ___ ___ ___   ___ ___ ___ ___ ___ ___ ___ ___
 1   2   3   3 15 13   6   1   7 14   8 17   9 10   1 11

___ ___ ___ ___ ___   ___   ___ ___ ___ !
12   6   2   8   5   16   11 17   4

YOUR BODY AND BODY IMAGE

The human body is the best picture of the human soul.

Ludwig Wittgenstein

NAME   DATE

What Is Your Body Type?

Human bodies, like cars, can be categorized into types. Examine the three body types below and circle the name of the one that best describes you.

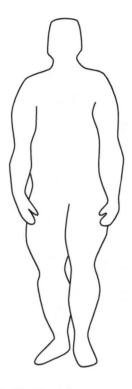 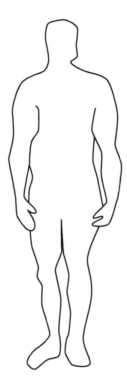 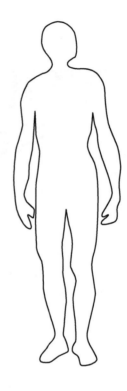

ENDOMORPH

You gain fat more easily than the other two body types.

You have full shoulders, prominent hips and thighs.

You find it difficult to stay thin.

Your body is naturally rounder than the other two types.

MESOMORPH

Your body is naturally muscular.

It takes little effort for you to get into and stay in shape.

Your body has strong arms and legs, dominant shoulders, and narrow hips.

ECTOMORPH

Your body is naturally tall and thin.

You may look like you are in better shape than you actually are.

Your body has long arms and legs and slim hips.

You have trouble putting on either fat or muscle.

Calculate Your BMI

In order to determine whether or not your weight is healthy for a person of your height, you need to apply a scientific measurement called the Body Mass Index (or BMI).

To determine your BMI, put an X on Scale A marking your height. Then put an X on Scale B marking your weight. Draw a line joining the two Xs and extend this line so that it meets Scale C.

Your BMI is _____.

- If your BMI is less than 20, you are underweight.

- If your BMI is between 20 and 25, then your weight is perfect for your height.

- If your BMI is between 25 and 27, then you are within an acceptable range, but you may want to keep an eye on your eating habits and fitness patterns.

- If your BMI is above 27, then you may want to look into healthy methods of losing weight.

Scale A	Scale B	Scale C
6'6"	380	40
	370	
6'5"	360	39
	350	38
6'4"	340	
	330	37
6'3"	320	36
	310	
6'2"	300	35
	290	
6'1"	280	34
	270	33
	260	
6'0"	250	32
	240	
5'11"	230	31
	220	
5'10"	210	30
	200	
5'9"	190	29
	180	28
5'8"	175	
	170	27
5'7"	165	26
	160	
5'6"	155	25
	150	
5'5"	145	24
	140	23
5'4"	135	
	130	22
5'3"	125	21
	120	
5'2"	115	20
	110	
5'1"	105	19
	100	18
5'0"	95	
	90	17

height in feet/inches   weight in lbs.   BMI

Source: This chart was adapted from *Healthy Weights: A New Way of Looking at Your Weight and Height* (Ontario, Canada: Ontario Ministry of Health), 1991.

Body Image and You

Each body is unique and all people have parts of their body they like and parts they dislike. Think about your body. What parts do you like, and what parts do you wish you could change?

Complete the chart below. If you like how the body part mentioned looks on you, then put a check mark in the column LIKE. If you dislike how the body part looks on you, but have accepted the way it looks, put a check mark in the column DISLIKE BUT ACCEPT. If you really dislike the way the body part looks on your body and would love to change it, put a check mark in the column DISLIKE.

Body Parts	Like	Dislike But Accept	Dislike
HAIR			
EYES			
NOSE			
EARS			
MOUTH			
CHEEKS			
FOREHEAD			
NECK			
SHOULDERS			
UPPER ARMS			
ELBOWS			
LOWER ARMS			
WRISTS			
HANDS			
FINGERS			
FINGER NAILS			
CHEST			
STOMACH			
BELLYBUTTON			
WAIST			
BACK			
BUTTOCKS			
LEGS			
KNEECAPS			
ANKLES			
FEET			
TOES			
TOE NAILS			

NAME DATE

Body Image and You: Questions

After completing the chart entitled Body Image and You, answer these questions.

1. Which column did you have the most check marks in: LIKE, DISLIKE BUT ACCEPT, or DISLIKE? _____

2. What does the phrase *body image* mean to you? _____
   _____

3. Would you consider that you have a positive body image? _____

4. If you don't have a positive body image, what factors or reasons have given you a negative body image? _____
   _____

5. What can you do to improve your body image? _____
   _____

6. If you do have a positive body image, what factors or reasons have given you a positive body image? _____
   _____

7. What can you do to ensure that you maintain a positive body image for the rest of your life? _____

8. Do you think most Americans have a positive or negative body image, and why?
   _____

9. How can you help people with negative body images feel better about themselves?
   _____
   _____

NAME

DATE

Body Images and the Sexes

In general, women worry about different things than men do, particularly when it comes to body image. Think about the two genders. How do their feelings about body image differ?

In the space below list five things that many women worry about in terms of their bodies and then five things that men tend to worry about in terms of their bodies.

WHAT WOMEN WORRY ABOUT
1.
2.
3.
4.
5.

WHAT MEN WORRY ABOUT
1.
2.
3.
4.
5.

Cosmetic Plastic Surgery

Many Americans choose to eliminate wrinkles, make their lips fuller, make their noses smaller, or get their tummies tucked through cosmetic plastic surgery. The word *plastic* originates from the Greek word *plastikos,* meaning to form or to mold. Cosmetic plastic surgery corrects physical defects or beautifies body parts.

What are your thoughts on cosmetic plastic surgery? Would you ever get cosmetic plastic surgery? Why or why not?

_____

_____

_____

Complete the multiple-choice test below to learn more about cosmetic plastic surgery. The information is based on statistics published in 2000 by the American Society for Aesthetic Plastic Surgery (ASAPS).

1. According to ASAPS, how many cosmetic surgical and nonsurgical procedures were done in the United States in 2000?

   a. 100,000

   b. Over 1 million

   c. Over 5 million

   d. Over 25 million

2. Which age group had the most cosmetic procedures?

   a. People ages 12 to 18

   b. People ages 19 to 34

   c. People ages 35 to 50

   d. People ages 51 to 65

3. Which race or ethnicity has proportionately the most cosmetic procedures?

   a. Caucasians

   b. Hispanics

   c. African Americans

   d. Asian Americans

4. According to the ASAPS, cosmetic plastic surgery is:

   a. less popular today than in the past.

   b. more popular today than it was even a year ago.

   c. about as common today as it was a year ago.

Body-Parts Connections

Connect the body part with the definition of what it does by drawing a line from the body part to the definition.

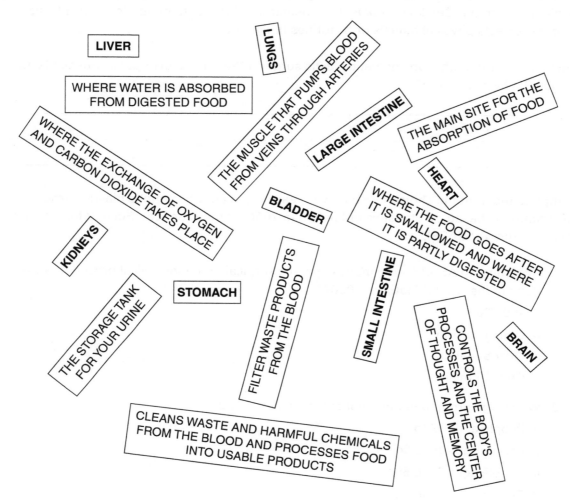

LIVER

LUNGS

WHERE WATER IS ABSORBED FROM DIGESTED FOOD

THE MUSCLE THAT PUMPS BLOOD FROM VEINS THROUGH ARTERIES

LARGE INTESTINE

THE MAIN SITE FOR THE ABSORPTION OF FOOD

WHERE THE EXCHANGE OF OXYGEN AND CARBON DIOXIDE TAKES PLACE

HEART

BLADDER

WHERE THE FOOD GOES AFTER IT IS SWALLOWED AND WHERE IT IS PARTLY DIGESTED

KIDNEYS

THE STORAGE TANK FOR YOUR URINE

STOMACH

FILTER WASTE PRODUCTS FROM THE BLOOD

SMALL INTESTINE

CONTROLS THE BODY'S PROCESSES AND THE CENTER OF THOUGHT AND MEMORY

BRAIN

CLEANS WASTE AND HARMFUL CHEMICALS FROM THE BLOOD AND PROCESSES FOOD INTO USABLE PRODUCTS

Body-Parts Vocabulary

Listed below are body parts followed by four scientific terms. One of the four terms names a part of that body part. For example, let's say that the body part is LEG. Choose the one of the following four terms that names something that's a part of the leg: clavicle, gastrocnemius, frontal lobe, periodontium.

The answer is gastrocnemius, which is a major muscle in the leg. In contrast, the clavicle is a bone in the shoulder, the frontal lobe is part of the brain, and the periodontium is the area around the tooth.

For each group of words below, circle the one that names a part of that body part.

EAR

Cornea

Cochlea

Cerebrum

Crown

FEMALE BREAST

Milk duct

Urethra

Ventricle

Eustachian tube

HEART

Urethra

Periodontium

Right atrium

Iris

EYE

Retina

Ossicles

Diaphragm

Ulna

BRAIN

Nasal cavity

Soleus

Patella

Frontal lobe

ARM

Stapes

Biceps

Ureters

Rectus abdominus

MOUTH

Ureters

Cervix

Salivary glands

Scrotum

FOOT

Larynx

Metatarsals

Incus

Pancreas

HAND

Spleen

Prostate

Metacarpals

Larynx

Muscle Word Search

For each clue determine which muscle is being described and write the name of the muscle in the space provided. Then find the muscle in the word search. The answers can be found forward, backward, and diagonally.

1. _____ This group of muscles is at the back of your thighs.

2. _____ You sit on this muscle (two words).

3. _____ This muscle is one of the two muscles in the calf.

4. _____ We nickname these our "abs" (two words).

5. _____ Found at your temple, this muscle helps you clench your teeth.

6. _____ When you bend your elbows and clench your fists, these muscles bulge.

7. _____ These muscles are found at the back of your upper arms.

8. _____ This muscle at the back of your calf helps steady your legs when you are standing.

9. _____ This muscle wraps around your ribs in the middle of your upper back (two words).

10. _____ These muscles are located in the front of the thigh.

11. _____ These muscles can be found in the middle of your upper back.

12. _____ These muscles near your chest area are often nicknamed "pecs."

G	L	U	T	E	U	S	M	A	X	I	M	U	S	G	L	P
L	N	X	L	O	S	O	L	E	U	S	W	A	U	C	X	E
U	T	I	T	X	T	P	U	V	W	E	K	B	I	V	W	C
T	R	A	R	O	S	U	E	I	F	J	D	F	M	V	A	T
S	A	P	I	T	L	Z	V	C	R	S	I	S	E	T	U	O
P	M	A	C	B	S	Q	O	G	I	Y	C	H	N	N	L	R
E	O	A	E	E	N	M	L	L	C	B	A	X	C	G	K	A
C	V	D	P	L	M	I	A	D	K	Q	U	A	O	T	R	L
I	I	B	S	B	R	R	C	H	E	R	E	F	R	O	S	I
R	U	R	Q	D	O	F	P	W	D	L	R	M	T	U	M	S
D	T	R	A	P	E	Z	I	U	S	Q	U	V	S	S	X	T
A	H	A	M	K	G	H	N	O	W	I	J	S	A	R	K	B
U	V	E	I	U	M	V	T	J	N	P	Z	O	G	L	A	Y
Q	T	E	X	T	E	R	N	A	L	O	B	L	I	Q	U	E
S	I	N	I	M	O	D	B	A	S	U	T	C	E	R	K	Q

Right Muscle, Right Exercise

Each muscle listed below is followed by a list of four exercises. One of these exercises will not strengthen the muscle named. While some exercises strengthen more than one muscle group, certain exercises isolate specific muscles. Draw a line through the one exercise in each group of four that is least effective for the named muscle.

TRICEPS (Back of Arm)

Triceps pull-down

Partial sit-up

Bench press

Lying triceps extension

QUADRICEPS (Thigh)

Lunge

Leg press

Squat

Concentration curl

ABDOMINALS (Stomach)

Preacher curl

Partial sit-up

Bent knee sit-up

Leg raises (bent knees)

DELTOIDS (Front Shoulder)

Dumbbell press

Bench press

Lunge

Military press

PECTORALS (Chest)

Push-up

Incline press

Bent arm pull-over

Lunge

ERECTORS (Lower Back)

Straight-leg dead lift

Dumbbell press

Regular dead lift

Back hyperextension

LATISSIMUS DORSI (Back)

Pull-down

Bent-over row

Seated row

Squat

GLUTEALS (Buttocks)

Squat

Lunge

Preacher curl

Power clean

NAME _____   DATE _____

The Human Skeleton Crossword

Across

3. The two bones of the lower arm are the _____ and the radius.

5. Our shoulders are made up of two bones: the scapula (the shoulder blade) and the _____ (the collarbone).

7. The spine of the vertebral column consists of 24 _____.

9. Two bones make up the lower leg. They are the _____ and the fibula.

10. These fibrous tissues join skeleton muscles to bones: _____.

12. All the bones in the upper foot are called the _____.

13. The 206 bones in the body make up the human _____.

16. The bones that make up the middle part of the foot are called the _____.

17. The jawbone is called the _____.

18. If you fall on your knees, you fall on this bone: _____.

19. This bone in your leg is the longest and heaviest bone in your body: _____.

20. The Latin name for this bone means basin because the bone is bowl-shaped: _____.

Down

1. These fibrous tissues join one bone to another across a joint: _____.

2. If you break your upper arm, you've broken this bone: _____.

4. The palm of your hand is made up of the _____.

5. Our ears and the tips of our noses aren't made of bones but of flexible _____.

6. Its job is to house and protect the brain: _____.

8. If you break your toe or finger, you have broken a _____.

11. The place where two bones meet is called a _____.

13. The bony plate in the middle of the chest is the _____.

14. The small bones of the hand are the _____.

15. We have 12 pairs of _____ that protect vital organs such as the heart and the lungs.

Here is a word bank to choose from:

vertebrae	joint	cranium	phalange	tibia	femur
cartilage	humerus	clavicle	ulna	ribs	metacarpals
pelvis	tendons	carpals	patella	skeleton	metatarsals
tarsals	mandible	ligaments	sternum		

Female Reproductive System Vocabulary

Choose the correct term from the list below and write it beside the appropriate definition.

CERVIX	HYMEN	MONS PUBIS
CLITORIS	LABIA (INNER AND OUTER)	UTERUS
FALLOPIAN TUBES	VAGINAL OPENING	OVARIES

1. _____ The soft tissue, which is covered with pubic hair, that serves as a protective pillow for the reproductive organs

2. _____ The opening of the vagina

3. _____ The narrow lower end part of the uterus

4. _____ The tubes from the ovary to the uterus through which the egg moves

5. _____ The pear-shaped organ that holds the developing fetus

6. _____ Where eggs are stored and hormones are produced

7. _____ A highly sensitive organ located above the urethral opening (when stimulated may induce orgasm)

8. _____ The thin membrane stretching across the vaginal opening

9. _____ The fold of skin that protects and surrounds the opening of the vagina

NAME _____   DATE

Male Reproductive System Vocabulary

Choose the correct term from the list below and write it beside the appropriate definition.

COWPER'S GLANDS	PROSTATE GLAND	TESTICLES
EPIDIDYMIS	SCROTUM	URETHRA
PENIS	SEMINAL VESICLES	VAS DEFERENS

1. _____ Two tubes that serve as a passageway for sperm, sending them to the ejaculatory duct

2. _____ The male sex organ that becomes enlarged and erect when the man is sexually aroused

3. _____ This gland produces a milky fluid that helps sperm live longer

4. _____ The tube through which both semen and urine leave the body

5. _____ The place where sperm and testosterone is produced

6. _____ A pair of glands that add a nourishing fluid to the sperm

7. _____ A tube on the surface of each testicle that stores and transports sperm

8. _____ The small glands located on either side of the urethra that secrete a lubricating fluid

9. _____ The sac that holds the testicles

NAME   DATE

The Respiratory System Matching Exercise

The respiratory system is vital to human existence. Basically, the respiratory system consists of the body parts that control breathing. Column A presents a list of terms related to the respiratory system. Match each term in Column A with its proper definition in Column B by writing the number of the definition in the space preceding the term in Column A.

COLUMN A

____ alveoli

____ bronchi

____ carbon dioxide

____ lung

____ nose (and nasal cavity)

____ oxygen

____ pharynx

____ pulmonary veins

____ respiratory system

____ trachea

COLUMN B

1. This element is essential for any animal to live.

2. This is the name for the body parts that are in charge of breathing.

3. The opening through which we inhale oxygen. As we inhale, tiny hairs catch small specks of dirt and stop them from going any farther.

4. This is the gas given off from the lungs that is breathed out during the respiratory process.

5. Air goes from the nose through this to the larynx (voice box) and the windpipe.

6. Air travels through this organ (also called the windpipe) into two tubes called the bronchi.

7. There are two of these. One enters the right lung, while the other enters the left lung. The air that passes through the windpipe divides to one of these two branches.

8. From the bronchial tree, the air moves into these tiny, thin-walled sacs in the lungs where the exchange of oxygen and carbon dioxide takes place.

9. This organ, located in the chest, is the size of a football. It removes carbon dioxide from the blood and exchanges it with oxygen. (There are two of these.)

10. The blood leaves the lungs with oxygen and travels through these to the heart.

NAME   DATE

The Digestion Puzzle

Listed below are the steps of food digestion, but they are in the wrong order. Put the steps into correct order by putting a number on the blank space beside each one: 1 means this is the first step, 2 the second step, and so on.

_____ The food leaves the stomach a bit at a time.

_____ The tongue helps push the food to the back of the mouth so it can move into the esophagus.

_____ Food enters the mouth.

_____ The food enters the small intestine, where the digestive juices finish breaking down the food.

_____ During chewing, saliva is squirted into the mouth to help soften the food.

_____ Food waste goes to the large intestines where it forms feces.

_____ Teeth begin to break down the food.

_____ The food moves from the esophagus into the stomach, where the food mixes with acids from the stomach.

_____ The chewed food is swallowed and travels down the esophagus.

The Sun and Your Skin

Because of air pollution and the depletion of the ozone layer, people need to worry about skin cancer. Complete the following survey to determine your skin's sensitivity to the sun.

	Number of Points
1. If you have tanned in a tanning booth or have used a sun lamp more than 10 times a year, give yourself 10 points.	
2. If your hair is naturally blonde or red in color, give yourself 10 points.	
3. If you spend a lot of time outdoors each week, give yourself 10 points.	
4 If there is a history of skin cancer in your family, give yourself 10 points.	
5. If you have lots of freckles or get freckles easily, give yourself 10 points.	
6. If you have had at least 10 serious sunburns that developed blisters, give yourself 10 points.	
7. If you usually burn before you get a tan, give yourself 10 points.	
8. If your eyes are blue or green in color, give yourself 10 points.	
9. If you have lots of moles on your body, give yourself 10 points.	
10. If you have lived (or currently live) or vacation regularly in a tropical climate, give yourself 10 points.	

TOTAL SCORE _____

If your score is . . .

80 to 100: You are at a high risk for skin cancer and should do everything possible to protect your skin from the sun.

40 to 70: You are at an increased risk. You still need to protect your skin from the sun.

0 to 30: You are at a small risk. However, you should still be aware when out in the sun and practice skin protection.

LIST A FEW WAYS YOU CAN PROTECT YOUR SKIN FROM THE SUN: _____

_____

_____

_____

Genetics and Your Health

Scientists have proven that some diseases are hereditary, which means they can be passed down from one generation to the next. Complete this family tree with as much health information as you are able to obtain about your biological family. Include information like poor eyesight or the tendency to get migraines, as well as major illnesses such as lung cancer and multiple sclerosis. If the relative is deceased, indicate how he or she died.

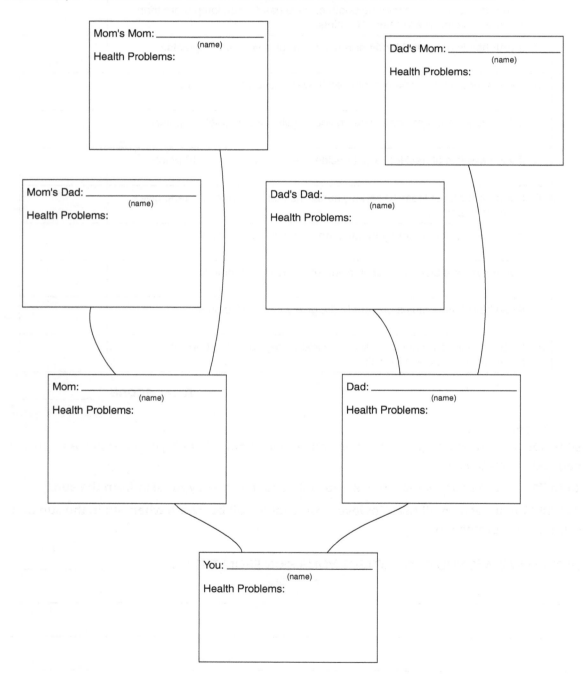

NAME

Dr. Doctor's Magic Square

If your family doctor sent you to an oncologist, would you know what an oncologist specializes in? This vocabulary exercise will help you learn the specific areas of expertise for various medical specialists.

Match the type of doctor named in Column A with his or her area of expertise in Column B. Write the number in the appropriate box in the magic square below. The sum of the numbers will be the same across each row, down each column, and along the diagonals. This sum is the magic number.

Column A: Type of Doctors

a. AUDIOLOGIST

b. CARDIOLOGIST

c. CHIROPRACTOR

d. DERMATOLOGIST

e. ENDODONTIST

f. GYNECOLOGIST

g. NEUROLOGIST

h. ONCOLOGIST

i. OPTHALMOLOGIST

j. OPTOMETRIST

k. PEDIATRICIAN

l. PEDODONTIST

m. PODIATRIST

n. PROSTHETIST

o. DIAGNOSTIC RADIOLOGIST

p. UROLOGIST

Column B: Definitions

1. Specializes in diseases of the urinary tract.

2. Specializes in the heart and heart disease.

3. Specializes in relief of back pain by way of manipulations.

4. Specializes in foot diseases.

5. Specializes in diseases of dental pulp and surrounding tissues (such as root canal).

6. Specializes in the treatment of children's diseases.

7. Specializes in examining eyes and prescribing corrective lenses.

8. Specializes in the treatment of cancer and malignant tumors.

9. Specializes in diseases of the eye.

10. Specializes in diseases of the nervous system.

11. Specializes in caring for women's reproductive health and related diseases.

12. Dentist who specializes in the care of children's teeth.

13. Specializes in skin and skin diseases.

14. Specializes in the construction of artificial limbs.

15. One who practices diagnosis using X rays and ultrasound.

16. Specializes in hearing.

a	b	c	d
e	f	g	h
i	j	k	l
m	n	o	p

The magic number is: _____.

NAME _____   DATE

What Makes You Ill?

Living things like bacteria and viruses, which reside in our bodies, sometimes make us ill. Bacteria are so small that you need a microscope to see them. Most of the time bacteria in your body are harmless; however, if your body isn't working properly, bacteria may invade parts of your body that aren't working well and make you sick. Viruses are smaller than bacteria and cannot live on their own. They can only survive by living inside the cells of other living things.

For each disease or illness, write VIRUS in the blank space if a virus causes the illness or write BACTERIA if bacteria cause the illness.

1. Scarlet fever _____

2. Common cold _____

3. Salmonella food poisoning _____

4. The flu _____

5. Measles _____

6. Whooping cough _____

7. Mumps _____

8. Cholera _____

9. Smallpox _____

10. AIDS _____

Five Diseases and Conditions
That May Affect Teens

Here is a chart presenting the definitions of, causes, symptoms, and treatments for five diseases that affect some teens. Unfortunately, the information is all mixed up. Although the causes are shown in the correct column, no cause is in the correct row for the named disease; definitions are also in wrong rows. Each illness has a number. Put each number in the box that correctly provides the illness's definition, cause, symptom, or treatment.

Disease	Definition	Cause	Symptom	Treatment
Asthma (1)	This is a life-threatening condition in which a person's body loses the ability to turn sugar into useable energy.	There is no single cause of the disease. Some things that trigger a seizure are flashing lights, stress, lack of sleep, & low sugar levels.	Symptoms vary from person to person but a ring-like rash occurs in 60% of the cases. Fatigue, chills, or a headache may accompany the rash. If not treated, this disease can develop serious symptoms like blindness or memory loss, etc.	This disease can be treated through antibiotics.
Diabetes (2)	This is a condition that affects the nervous system. Many people with the condition have sudden attacks or seizures.	This is not passed as easily as some viruses. The virus is found in mucus and saliva and so is often passed through kissing.	Symptoms may vary but the most significant symptom is difficulty breathing, a tight, dry cough, and wheezing.	Although this condition cannot be cured, it can be controlled with anticonvulsant medication.
Epilepsy (3)	This disease affects the respiratory system. It occurs when the airways become narrow or blocked resulting in breathing difficulties.	Bacteria transmitted through the bite of an infected deer tick cause the disease.	Other symptoms are a fever, sore throat, enlarged lymph nodes, and an enlarged spleen.	People with type 1 can use insulin to control this, while type 2 can control the condition by altering diet and oral medication.
Lyme Disease (4)	This is an infection caused by the Epstein-Barr virus.	Physical activity, anxiety, stress, smoke, pollen, or dust may trigger an attack or reaction.	Some people may have no symptoms. However, some symptoms are: - frequent urination - unusual thirst - unexplained weight loss - fatigue - blurred vision	It cannot be cured, but the virus usually goes away on its own in about a month.
Mononucleosis (5)	This bacterial disease was first diagnosed in Connecticut in 1975. It is common in the northeast States.	The cause is unknown although childhood infections and heredity may cause this. With type 2, obesity, genetics, and aging are significant factors.	Seizures are the most common symptom.	There is no cure, but drugs can control an attack.

NAME

DATE

Basic First-Aid Crossword

Use the words in the crossword word bank to complete the crossword puzzle. Note: There are more words in the bank than you need to complete the puzzle.

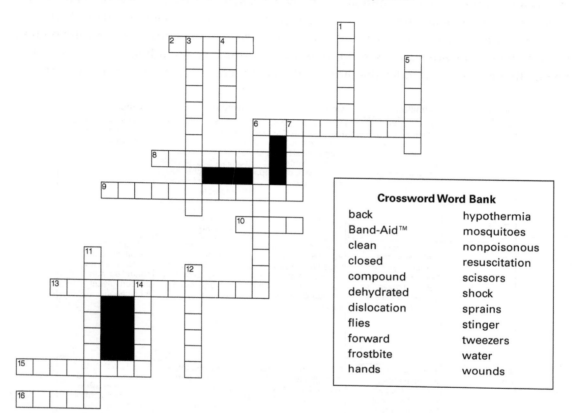

Crossword Word Bank

back	hypothermia
Band-Aid™	mosquitoes
clean	nonpoisonous
closed	resuscitation
compound	scissors
dehydrated	shock
dislocation	sprains
flies	stinger
forward	tweezers
frostbite	water
hands	wounds

Across

2. Acute stress reaction is also known as _____.

6. If you haven't had much to drink and you're thirsty, you may be _____.

8. The accidental overstretching of a tendon or ligament causes _____.

9. Before you treat a snake bite, determine if the snake was poisonous or _____.

10. If you get a nosebleed, do not lean your head _____.

13. CPR—known as cardiopulmonary _____—may help you save a life.

15. With an open or _____ fracture, the bone protrudes through the skin.

16. _____ can spread bacteria that cause dysentery, typhoid, and cholera.

Down

1. If a bee stings you, immediately remove the _____.

3. The body's failure to maintain a body temperature of 98 degrees Fahrenheit is called _____.

4. If you have an open wound, the first thing you should do is _____ the wound.

5. A closed fracture has no open _____.

6. A _____ is the separation of bone joints, which causes the bones to move out of proper alignment.

7. Before cooking, wash your _____.

11. These insects carry malaria: _____.

12. Found in a first-aid kit, this should be put on small cuts and wounds: _____.

14. There are two types of fractures: open and _____.

Diagnose the Emergency

Listed below are some health emergencies. For each scenario, determine what is wrong with the person and how you could help.

PERSON A

You come across a person in the cafeteria who is very pale, or even bluish in color. When you ask him what is the matter, he can't speak and gestures wildly toward his food.

What is the problem? _____

How can you help this person? _____

_____

_____

PERSON B

You and a friend are walking through the woods. Your friend hollers and then shows you her arm. There is a red mark on her arm and some swelling. You can also see a stinger still sticking in the skin.

What is the problem? _____

How can you help this person? _____

_____

_____

PERSON C

You're playing baseball in July and the temperature has risen to 100 degrees Fahrenheit. While sitting on the bench waiting for your turn at bat, you notice that your team's pitcher has a red face, is perspiring, and complains of dizziness and nausea.

What is the problem? _____

How can you help this person? _____

_____

_____

Preventing Cardiovascular Disease

Any disease of the heart or of the blood vessels that lead from the heart to other body parts is called cardiovascular disease. Heart attacks (which occur when an insufficient amount of blood flows to the heart) and strokes (which occur when an insufficient amount of blood flows to the brain) are the most common cardiovascular diseases.

Doctors have determined a number of factors (some of which are listed below) that increase a person's chance of developing a cardiovascular disease. People have no control over some of these factors but can control others. In the space provided after each factor, write the word UNCONTROLLABLE if this factor cannot be controlled and write CONTROL-LABLE if this factor can be controlled.

1. Not enough exercise _____

2. Too much stress _____

3. Gender _____

4. Smoking _____

5. Poor eating habits _____

6. Overweight _____

7. Increased age _____

8. Excessive alcohol consumption _____

9. Family history of cardiovascular disease _____

10. High blood pressure _____

A Fitness Survey

Complete this survey in order to learn more about your fitness habits.

	Rarely	Often	Always
1. Do you work out so that you increase your heart rate for 45 minutes three times a week?	1	2	3
2. Do you have a regular weight-lifting routine?	1	2	3
3. Do you exercise just for fun?	1	2	3
4. Do you participate in team sports?	1	2	3
5. Do you participate in individual sports?	1	2	3
6. Do you participate in sports that you can enjoy as you age?	1	2	3
7. Do you participate in sports that don't cost a lot of money?	1	2	3
8. Do you need a friend or companion with you when you exercise?	1	2	3
9. Do you participate in sports that don't require much equipment?	1	2	3
10. Do you participate in sports with your family?	1	2	3

In the space below, summarize in a few sentences what this survey revealed about your fitness habits and attitudes about fitness.

_____

_____

_____

_____

NAME

DATE

Components of Fitness

Here is a list of the components of fitness along with their definitions. For each component of fitness, circle the action, exercise, or activity that could best improve it. Then, in the space provided, list other activities and exercises that would improve that specific component.

1. CARDIOVASCULAR ENDURANCE is the ability to continue strenuous activity that stresses the heart and respiratory systems for a long period of time. What activity best improves cardiovascular endurance?

   a. Doing a cartwheel

   b. Throwing a shot put

   c. Skipping rope for 15 minutes

   d. Standing on a balance beam on one foot

   What other exercises can you do to improve cardiovascular endurance? _____

   _____

2. MUSCULAR STRENGTH refers to the maximum tension that a muscle can exert in a single contraction. What activity best improves muscular strength?

   a. Standing long jump

   b. Shuttle run

   c. Running around the bases in baseball

   d. Doing splits

   What other exercises can you do to improve muscular strength? _____

   _____

3. MUSCULAR ENDURANCE refers to the ability of a muscular group to perform repeated contractions over a period of time. What activity best improves muscular endurance?

   a. Lifting weights, having high repetition with low weight

   b. Running long jump

   c. Dancing

   d. Diving into a pool

   What other exercises can you do to improve muscular endurance? _____

   _____

4. FLEXIBILITY is the range of motion of a joint or series of joints. Which activity best improves flexibility?

   a. Swimming 20 laps in a pool

   b. Sit-and-reach exercises

   c. Participating in an aerobics class

   d. Throwing a football

   What other exercises can you do to improve flexibility? _____

   _____

Copyright © 2004 by John Wiley & Sons, Inc.

Anaerobic Energy, Aerobic Energy, and DOM

Two distinct systems provide muscles with energy to sustain or repeat intense effort:

- ANAEROBIC ENERGY: This requires no oxygen. It uses energy stored in the cells for fuel. It is the main energy source for activities lasting up to 10 seconds—for example, the 100-meter sprint.

- AEROBIC ENERGY: This requires oxygen. It uses fats and carbohydrates for fuel and is the main source of energy for activities lasting more than two minutes—for example, a 10-mile cross-country run.

Determine which energy systems the following activities use and write this in the space provided.

1. Racing up a flight of 15 steps _____

2. Running in the Boston Marathon _____

3. Vaulting in gymnastics _____

4. Competing in a 25-meter swimming race _____

5. Going cross-country skiing for an afternoon _____

Delayed Onset Muscle (DOM) Soreness

DOM is caused by strenuous, unaccustomed exercise that may give a person pain in certain muscles. Often the pain shows up after the exercise.

What are three ways to prevent DOM?

1. _____

2. _____

3. _____

NAME

DATE

Keeping Fit Without Doing Aerobics

Most people would prefer to have a fit body than an unfit body, yet the percentage of Americans who are out of shape keeps increasing. Nonetheless, with just a minor adjustment in many people's habits, they could be in better shape.

Here are a series of incomplete sentences. Complete each sentence by writing a better alternative for getting your body into better shape.

Instead of changing channels on the TV with the remote, you could _____

_____

Instead of getting a drive to school, you could _____

Instead of renting a movie, you could _____

Instead of talking on the phone with a friend, you could _____

Instead of playing a computer game, you could _____

Instead of going through the drive-through, you could _____

Instead of cutting the grass with a riding lawn mower, you could _____

Instead of taking a golf cart when you play golf, you could _____

Instead of getting on the Internet to check out which movies are playing at the theater down

the street, you could _____

Instead of taking the elevators four floors, you could _____

SELF-ESTEEM AND KNOWING YOURSELF

This above all: to thine own self be true.

William Shakespeare

NAME _____   DATE

What's in a Name?

Everyone has a name and our names say a lot about us. Many names have interesting stories behind them or tell something about our cultural heritage and background.

Using your own name and what you know about it, complete this worksheet.

What is your first name? _____

Why did your parents give you this name? Do you know the meaning of your first name? Is there an interesting story behind this name? _____

_____

_____

_____

What is your middle name? _____

Why did your parents give you this name? Do you know the meaning of this name? Is there an interesting story behind the choosing of this name? _____

_____

_____

_____

What is your last name? _____

Where does your last name come from? Do you know any interesting stories about your ancestors or anyone else who shares your last name? _____

_____

_____

_____

I Am

Follow the instructions below to help you complete the poem "I Am" and make it a poem about you.

Line 1: I am (write your first name).

Line 2: I am the child of (write the full names of your parents).

Line 3: I am the grandchild of (write the full names of your four grandparents).

Line 4: I am the sibling of (write the first names of your brothers and sisters, if any).

Line 5: I am the friend of (write the names of a few of your friends).

Line 6: I am (write three descriptive words that describe you).

Line 7: I am a (write something that you do well—for example, I am a hockey player).

Line 8: I am a resident of (write the name of the city or town in which you live).

Line 9: I am (write your citizenship—for example, American).

I am _____

I am the child of _____

I am the grandchild of _____

_____

I am the sibling of _____

_____

I am the friend of _____

I am _____

I am a _____

I am a resident of _____

I am _____

NAME   DATE

Graffiti You

Imagine you are given a can of spray paint and told to spray your bedroom walls with quotations, sayings, and so on that reveal aspects of you. Unfortunately, we are not giving you a free can of spray paint; however, we are giving you a blank box to treat like your bedroom wall where you can write quotations, sayings, slogans, and so on that describe and reveal your likes, passions, and personality. A sample has been done below.

"If you give up your dreams, you die."
GO FOR IT!
I love N.Y.
For those who aren't strong enough or tough enough for gymnastics, try football (Ha, ha!)
Judge Jackson Rocks!
S+D M+R
HUNTSVILLE HIGH IS THE PLACE TO BE
GO, BILLS, GO!

Now it's your turn.

The YOU Report Card

If you were a teacher, how would you grade yourself on the following traits: with an A, B, C, D, or F? Next to each grade, write a comment. Also, complete the questions at the bottom of the report card.

Traits	Grade	Comments
Considerate to Others		
Has a Positive Attitude		
Communicates Effectively (both verbally and in writing)		
Ability to Take on Leadership Roles (if necessary)		
Avoids Caving into Peer Pressure		
Comfortable and Welcoming When Meeting New People		
Open to and Accepting of Change		
Honest to Others		
Friendly		
Able to Take Initiative		

Which areas do you feel you need to improve in? What are you planning to do to make these improvements? _____

_____

_____

Which areas do you think you excel in? _____

_____

_____

What You Like to Do

The things you like to do, and who you do them with, say a lot about who you are.

- In Column A, list 10 things you like to do.
- In Column B, put an X beside the things you like to do with other people.
- In Column C, put an X beside the things you like to do alone.
- In Column D, put an X beside the things that cost money.
- In Column E, put an X beside the things you have done in the past week.
- In Column F, put an X beside the things you hope you will still be able to do in 20 years.

Column A	B	C	D	E	F
1.					
2.					
3.					
4.					
5.					
6.					
7.					
8.					
9.					
10.					

In the space below, write a few sentences explaining what you have learned about yourself from this exercise.

_____

_____

_____

_____

_____

You Are Where You Live

Where you live has a lot to do with your attitudes, values, worries, and beliefs. For example, if you live in certain countries or in certain parts of America you may be worried about getting enough to eat, while many people who live in more wealthy parts of the world are concerned about dieting. Your home state may also determine certain things about you. For example, if you live in North Dakota you may dream about competing in the winter Olympics, but if you live in Alabama you may dream about competing in the summer Olympics. As you complete this worksheet, consider where you live and how this location has shaped your thoughts, values, concerns, beliefs, passions, and worries.

In what **village, town, or city** do you live? _____

How has this village, town, or city shaped you? _____

_____

_____

_____

_____

In what **state** do you live? _____

How has this state influenced who you are? _____

_____

_____

_____

How has your **country** influenced your identity? _____

_____

_____

_____

NAME _____   DATE

What Would They Say About You?

No two people know you in exactly the same way. One of the reasons for this is that we tend to act differently around different groups and individuals. For example, when you go to the mall with your friends, you probably act differently from when you go to the mall with your grandmother.

Here is a list of people. In the space provided, write a sentence or two about how each person might describe you.

1. How might a police officer describe you? _____

   _____

2. How would your parents describe you? _____

   _____

3. How would your first-grade teacher describe you? _____

   _____

4. How would a religious leader describe you? _____

   _____

5. How would your best friend describe you? _____

   _____

6. How would your grandparents describe you? _____

   _____

7. How would a psychiatrist describe you? _____

   _____

8. How would a nutritionist describe you? _____

   _____

9. How would an athletic trainer (or a personal trainer) describe you? _____

   _____

Backing It Up with Examples

If you were asked to describe yourself, what adjectives would you use? In various situations—in job interviews, for example—you may be asked to describe your personality. The important thing to remember in these situations is not only to describe yourself accurately but also to find concrete examples to back up your description. For example, don't just say, "I'm cheap." Say, "I'm cheap and I demonstrated this when I took my girlfriend out on a date. She insisted we go to an expensive restaurant, and I pretended to forget my wallet so that she'd have to pay for the expensive meal."

Below is a list of adjectives. Choose three of these adjectives that best describe you and write these adjectives in the appropriate spaces in the chart. Then provide two concrete examples of things you have done that exemplify these adjectives.

enthusiastic	creative	reserved	daring	thoughtful
optimistic	athletic	communicative	caring	considerate
hard-working	musical	friendly	brave	intelligent
independent	mechanical	personable	fair	dramatic

Adjectives	Example #1	Example #2
Adjective #1 _____		
Adjective #2 _____		
Adjective #3 _____		

How Have These Outside Factors Shaped You?

Many of our needs, values, personality traits, and desires are shaped by the people and institutions around us. This exercise helps you examine how various outside factors have helped shape who you are. For each outside factor mentioned, describe how it has influenced you.

1. **Parents.** Your parents influence you in many different ways. How have your parents helped shape who you are?

   _____

   _____

2. **Friends.** Your peers also have a great influence on who you are. How have some of your friends helped shape who you are?

   _____

   _____

3. **School and extracurricular activities.** Your teachers, coaches, and community leaders can make an impact on what makes you unique. How have the people you know at school helped shape you?

   _____

   _____

4. **Media.** The TV shows you watch, the actors you admire, the computer games you play, and the films you see also influence your likes and dislikes. How has the media shaped you?

   _____

   _____

5. **This time in history.** The time period you live in also influences who you are. For example, if you grew up during the Great Depression of the 1930s, you might be quite different from the person you became growing up during the good economic times of the 1990s. How has this period in history helped shape you?

   _____

   _____

NAME

Personality and You

Your personality consists of all the traits that make you unique. A person's personality is the result of two things: heredity and environment.

Personality equation: PERSONALITY = HEREDITY + ENVIRONMENT

Think about your personality. In the space below brainstorm all the aspects of your personality that make you unique.

_____

_____

_____

_____

_____

Now categorize all of these traits by putting each one under either HEREDITY (if the trait is one you got from your parents or grandparents) or ENVIRONMENT (if the trait is one you developed on your own or with the influence of peer groups, culture, or the media).

HEREDITY	ENVIRONMENT

Personality and Physical, Mental, and Social Health

Your personality is a combination of your physical, mental, and social health. Physical health refers to how your body functions and your body image; mental health describes your values, emotions, and ability to deal with stress. Finally, social health refers to how you get along with others and interact with various types of people.

In the appropriate circle below, describe your physical, mental, and social health.

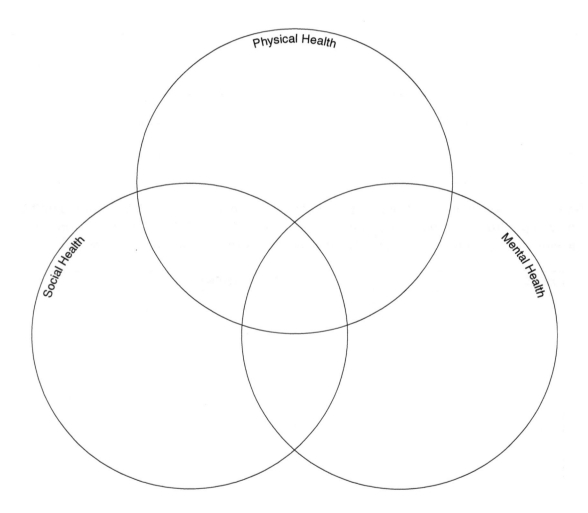

What's Your Personality?

Here are pairs of personality traits along with a description of each trait. For each pair, put a check mark in the space beside the one of the two that better describes you.

1. Are you . . .

   ____ Extroverted?

   Is sociable

   Is energized by being with people

   Does not like to be alone in a crowd

   ____ Introverted?

   Avoids crowds

   Needs time alone to reenergize

   Feels very "alone" in a crowd

2. Are you . . .

   ____ Logical?

   Thinks with the head

   Makes impersonal, objective decisions

   Sticks to rules and principles

   ____ Emotional?

   Thinks with the heart

   Decisions are more personal and subjective

   Feelings influence decisions

3. Are you . . .

   ____ A dreamer?

   Has a vivid imagination and likes to be creative

   Often daydreams and thinks of the future

   Avoids deadlines

   ____ A doer?

   Is practical and would rather spend time getting something done than thinking about doing it

   Is concerned about the present more than the future

   Sticks to deadlines

4. Are you . . .

   ____ A player?

   Work must be fun

   Is often late, doesn't meet deadlines

   Avoids making decisions

   ____ A worker?

   Whatever the work there is, it must be done before you can have fun.

   Meets deadlines

   Feels more comfortable after a decision is made

5. Do you see things as . . .

   ____ Black and white?

   Believes that issues and values are black and white and has established convictions

   ____ Gray?

   Sees all issues as shades of gray and tends to waver on thoughts and beliefs depending on individual situations

NAME   DATE

A, B, C, D Personality Types

There are many different tests and descriptions of the various personality types. You may have heard of some of these assessment tests. The Meyers-Briggs test, for example, divides people into 1 of 16 personality types. This worksheet divides people into 1 of 4 personality types. According to this test, you are either type A, B, C, or D. Read the descriptions of each personality type and put an X in the space next to the statements that best describe you. When you are finished, total the Xs. The type with the most Xs is your personality type.

TYPE A	**TYPE B**
_____ Thrives on change and fears routine	_____ Loves to have a good time
_____ Has an entrepreneurial streak	_____ Likes being the center of attention
_____ Enjoys taking risks and is driven to succeed	_____ Needs to be liked by others
_____ Is competitive and aggressive	_____ Tends to be talkative and outgoing
_____ Is impatient and is not a good listener	_____ Is relaxed and laid back
_____ Is persistent in getting what he/she wants	_____ Is not competitive or aggressive
TYPE C	**TYPE D**
_____ Takes everything seriously	_____ Doesn't like to take charge
_____ Thrives on details and accuracy	_____ Prefers a set of guidelines that he/she can follow
_____ Is predictable and dependable	_____ Is supportive of others
_____ Is loyal and patient	_____ Is punctual and consistent
_____ Is thoughtful and sensitive	_____ Is content and happy with life and him-/herself
_____ Likes facts	_____ Doesn't mind doing repetitive tasks

Birth Order and Personality

Many people believe that birth order determines aspects of a person's personality. Here is a brief summary of personality traits that some psychiatrists have attributed to each position in the birth order. Read this information and then in the space provided at the bottom of the page indicate your place in the birth order and whether or not this information describes you. (This information is from *Birth Order and You* by Dr. Ronald Richardson and Lois Richardson.)

Many first-born children:

- Are perfectionists, serious, careful, and conscientious

- Do not like surprises and prefer to be in control

- Often take leadership roles

Many second-born or middle children:

- Are more rebellious

- Break rules and question more in order to get noticed

- Sometimes feel left out and not respected

- Are often called "catch-up kids" because they are trying to catch up to their older sibling

- Are often the best adjusted as adults

Many youngest children:

- Love attention

- Are charming, outgoing, affectionate, and uncomplicated

- Are sometimes spoiled

- Sometimes feel left out and not taken seriously

Many only children:

- Are, like eldest children, overachievers

- Are, like youngest children, often pampered

- Are at ease with themselves and have high self-esteem

- Are sometimes smothered with attention by their parents

Where are you in the birth order? _____

Do you fit the description? Explain how you fit or do not fit the description for your birth-order position. _____

_____

_____

_____

Handwriting and Your Personality

The study of handwriting and what it tells about a person's personality is called *graphology.* Use this worksheet to examine what your handwriting reveals about you.

On the lines below sign your name and write the sentence: This is a great day. The sun is shining, and I feel amazing.

_____

_____

_____

Now use the information below to analyze what your writing says about you. (The source for this is *Handwriting Analysis Self-Taught* by Joel Engel.)

- People who forget the **t** bar or fail to dot the **i** are often careless and absentminded.
- If your writing goes above the top line, you are ambitious.
- If your sentence goes below the bottom line, you may be pessimistic and negative.
- Athletic types often have very long loops on letters like **f, g, y,** and **p**.

Now examine the slant of your writing:

- If the letters are fairly vertical, then you have lots of control over your emotions.
- If the letters slant toward the right, you may need and like communicating with others.
- If the letters slant toward the left, you may be an independent type who likes to be left alone.
- If the dot on your **i** is perfectly placed, you may be a perfectionist.
- If your letters connect like *this*, then you are both logical and practical.
- If your letters are disconnected like t h i s , then you are impractical and a daydreamer.
- Very wide spaces between words show that you are artistic.
- Timid and shy people write really small letters.
- Very large capitals at the beginning of a sentence indicate jealousy.
- Large writing and big letters indicate a happy person.
- If you make capital letters extra large, you may be overly confident.

Write your observations about your handwriting here. _____

_____

_____

_____

_____

Astrological Signs and Your Personality

Many people believe that the date of your birth and your astrology sign determines a lot about your personality. Look at your astrology sign below and the brief description of the people born under that sign. Then answer the question that follows.

Aquarius (Jan. 21-Feb. 19)
- Sometimes feels alienated or socially isolated.
- Creates a magic and fun atmosphere with people.
- Is warm and friendly but sometimes has trouble showing emotions.

Pisces (Feb. 20-Mar. 20)
- Goes "where the wind blows" and is considered a dreamer.
- His emotional sensitivity is expressed in the arts, particularly music and film.
- Is sometimes oversensitive and has a sense of martyrdom.

Aries (Mar. 21-Apr. 20)
- Has strong leadership traits.
- Is impulsive and short-tempered.
- Likes to be respected and hates people telling him what to do.
- Can be naive and romantic.

Taurus (Apr. 21-May 22)
- Is reluctant to initiate change.
- Enjoys relaxing, sensory pleasures.
- Sometimes materialistic or concerned about money.
- Likes security and stability.

Gemini (May 23-June 21)
- Is flexible, adaptable, and curious.
- Sometimes flighty, unreliable, and into too many things at once.
- Fun to be with, always willing to change, and doesn't take herself too seriously.

Cancer (June 22-July 22)
- Is loyal, sentimental, and holds onto the past.
- Sometimes feels vulnerable and can be oversensitive or possessive.
- Has a strong intuition and holds deep feelings.
- Has strong attachment to home and the familiar.

Leo (July 23-Aug. 22)
- Is warm, joyful, playful, and romantic.
- Sometimes is proud and self-important.
- Acts dramatically.
- Exerts an influence on others.

Virgo (Aug. 23-Sept. 22)
- Is a perfectionist who has a drive to work hard with a strong motivation to help others.
- Tends to analyze everything.
- Needs to organize.
- Is sometimes self-critical.

Libra (Sept. 23-Oct. 22)
- Is concerned about fairness and justice.
- Likes getting people to function well together.
- Is willing to compromise and desires peace at all cost.

Scorpio (Oct. 23-Nov. 21)
- Has great determination and endurance.
- Likes emotional security, which sometimes causes her to be jealous and passionate.
- Wants to control the unknown.
- Likes intense emotional relationships.

Sagittarius (Nov. 22-Dec. 22)
- Has a desire for the truth, a love of travel, and a need to learn about intellectual things.
- Dislikes trivial and superficial things.
- Is flexible and inspired by the mind and intellectual achievement.
- Is sometimes argumentative.

Capricorn (Dec. 23-Jan. 20)
- Is goal-oriented, practical, determined, and serious.
- Has a desire to reach the top based on hard work.
- Sometimes lacks emotional sensitivity and spontaneity.

Does your sign describe you? On a separate piece of paper, explain how it does or does not.

What Do You Value?

Values are qualities or conditions that are important to a person. Complete this survey by determining what you value in yourself. Circle the appropriate number based on the importance you assign to this attribute.

	Not Important				Very Important
1. To give 100 percent in everything I do	1	2	3	4	5
2. To be honest	1	2	3	4	5
3. To make lots of money	1	2	3	4	5
4. To be respected by my parents or guardians	1	2	3	4	5
5. To be respected by my friends	1	2	3	4	5
6. To do well in school	1	2	3	4	5
7. To do well in the activities I enjoy	1	2	3	4	5
8. To have a positive outlook	1	2	3	4	5
9. To try new things	1	2	3	4	5
10. To become a celebrity	1	2	3	4	5
11. To be healthy	1	2	3	4	5
12. To have lots of friends	1	2	3	4	5
13. To have a few friends, but ones who last a lifetime	1	2	3	4	5
14. To get the most out of every day	1	2	3	4	5
15. To learn new things	1	2	3	4	5

After completing this survey, what observations can you make about what you value?

_____

_____

_____

_____

_____

What Are Your Values . . . ?

In the space provided, write your answers to the questions.

1. If you found a hundred-dollar bill on the floor of a store, what would you do?

   _____

   _____

2. If you saw a friend stealing a pair of jeans from a store, what would you do?

   _____

   _____

3. If you were running late on your way to a job interview and witnessed a major car accident, what would you do?

   _____

   _____

4. If you hadn't had enough time to study for a major exam and during the exam you happened to sit next to the smartest kid in the class, what would you do?

   _____

   _____

5. If you saw your best friend's girlfriend (or boyfriend) kissing another boy (or girl), what would you do?

   _____

   _____

6. If you overheard your dad on the phone saying something you knew your mom would want to know but he probably would never tell her, what would you do?

   _____

   _____

7. If you were snooping in your sister's diary and found an entry in which she confessed to having an eating disorder, what would you do?

   _____

   _____

NAME _____   DATE

A Values Auction

At auctions people bid on items, and the highest bidder buys the item. Below is a list of "items." Imagine that you have been given $10,000 to spend at this silent values auction. For each item decide how much of your $10,000 you plan to bid. For some items, you may decide not to bid at all. You may not bid more than $10,000. After you are finished bidding, your class will get together to determine who has bid the most on each item. When you have completed this activity, look over this sheet and decide what your bids say about your personality and your values.

_____ A date with a celebrity of your choice

_____ An A+ average in all of your courses

_____ A year traveling around the world

_____ A chance to star in a movie

_____ A chance to be an Olympic athlete in the sport of your choice

_____ Good health for the rest of your life

_____ A complete designer wardrobe

_____ A happy, wonderful marriage

_____ The opportunity to raise healthy, great kids

_____ The job of your choice

_____ A fabulously fit body

_____ A chance to become a famous musician

_____ Enough financial security so that you never have to work again

_____ The ability to grant happiness to others

_____ The opportunity to become the president of the United States

_____ A publishing contract for a book you have written

_____ The ability to see into the future

_____ Eternal youth

_____ The chance to meet someone who has passed away

NAME

DATE

Weaknesses

Unfortunately, we all have weaknesses. We would all love to have perfect personalities, but as human beings, we have a few faults that could be improved. Maybe we worry too much, feel insecure, or try too hard to fit in. People can improve and work on their weaknesses. For example, people who are always late may want to set their watches back five minutes in order to help them get to places on time. Think about your own personal weaknesses. On the left-hand side of the chart, write your four greatest weaknesses. Then in the right-hand column, write a few strategies that might help you improve these weaknesses.

Weaknesses	Strategies to try to improve these weaknesses
1.	
2.	
3.	
4.	

A Few of Your Favorite Things

Your favorite things can reveal a lot about who you are and what you value. Answer the questions by listing your favorite things in each category. Then share this list with a friend or partner.

What (or who) is . . .

1. Your absolutely favorite possession? _____

2. Your favorite song? _____

3. Your favorite TV show? _____

4. Your favorite movie? _____

5. Your favorite book? _____

6. Your favorite magazine? _____

7. Your favorite gift? _____

8. Your favorite celebrity? _____

9. Your favorite article of clothing? _____

10. Your favorite food? _____

11. Your favorite childhood toy? _____

12. Your favorite city or town? _____

13. Your favorite piece of furniture? _____

14. Your favorite vacation spot? _____

15. Your favorite photograph? _____

16. Your favorite sport? _____

17. Your favorite computer or board game? _____

18. Your favorite color? _____

19. Your favorite month of the year? _____

221

Using Your Five Senses

Our five senses allow us to experience the world. Many people have things they especially love to see, hear, taste, touch, or smell. Think of your five senses and then answer the questions below.

1. What do you especially like to see? _____

_____

_____

_____

2. What do you especially like to hear? _____

_____

_____

_____

3. What do you especially like to taste? _____

_____

_____

_____

4. What do you especially like to touch? _____

_____

_____

_____

5. What do you especially like to smell? _____

_____

_____

_____

NAME   DATE

Highs/Lows and You

Life is full of highs and lows. None of us ever get everything we want out of life. A low is when something negative happens, and a high is when something positive happens. When you experience a low incident, it is important to remember that inevitably you will also experience one of life's highs as well. Think of the highs and lows for each time period mentioned below. (Try to think of a different high and low for each case.)

1. What was one of your highs yesterday? _____

_____

2. What was one of your lows yesterday? _____

_____

3. What was one of your highs last week? _____

_____

4. What was one of your lows last week? _____

_____

5. What was one of your highs last month? _____

_____

6. What was one of your lows last month? _____

_____

7. What was one of your highs last year? _____

_____

8. What was one of your lows last year? _____

_____

9. What was one of the biggest highs so far in your life? _____

_____

10. What was one of the biggest lows so far in your life? _____

_____

A Room with a Clue

We all need our own space. For many people this personal space is their bedroom, or if they share a bedroom, a part of a bedroom. Your personal space reveals a lot to other people about who you are, your likes, your passions, and your tastes. Use this worksheet to describe your personal space. (Use the back of this sheet if you need more room.)

1. What posters and pictures do you have on the walls of your bedroom or personal space?

   _____

   _____

   _____

2. In the box below, draw a floor plan of your bedroom.

   ┌───┐
   │   │
   │   │
   │   │
   │   │
   │   │
   │   │
   │   │
   │   │
   │   │
   └───┘

3. Describe your furniture and other aspects of your bedroom.

   _____

   _____

   _____

   _____

4. Describe some of the treasures that you have in your bedroom.

   _____

   _____

Cartoons, Colors, and Cars

Step 1: Begin this fun activity by responding to each of the following statements:

1. Name a cartoon character who is most like you:

   _____

2. Name a color that suits your personality:

   _____

3. Name a fruit or vegetable that best describes you:

   _____

4. Name a car that best describes you:

   _____

5. Name an animal that suits your personality:

   _____

Step 2: Submit this sheet back to your teacher. (Make sure your name is on it.) Your teacher will read some of these sheets aloud and have you and your classmates try to guess who the person is.

NAME _____   DATE

If . . .

If you won a million dollars, what is the first thing you would buy?

_____

If you could live anywhere in the world, where would you live?

_____

If you could visit any city in the world, which city would you visit?

_____

If you could change your first name, what would you change it to?

_____

If you could play any sport at an elite level, what would the sport be?

_____

If you could meet a celebrity, who would that celebrity be?

_____

If you could remain any age for 10 years, what would that age be?

_____

If you could become fluent in another language, what language would you choose?

_____

If you were president of the United States, who would you choose as your vice president?

_____

If you were the star of a romantic comedy film, who would you choose as your co-star?

_____

If you could work in any occupation, what occupation would you choose?

_____

If you could visit any place and time in history, what time and place would you choose?

_____

Answer Key

Note to teachers: Worksheets not shown here do not have set answers; student answers will vary. In Section 8, which is not shown here, student answers to all worksheets will vary.

Section 1: Drugs, Alcohol, and Smoking

2. What Drug Am I?

1. marijuana; 2. alcohol; 3. tobacco; 4. cocaine; 5. caffeine

3. Trends in Tobacco Use

1. c; 2. c; 3. d (in Nevada, 31.5 percent of the population smokes); 4. c (in Utah, 13.7 percent of the population smokes); 5. c; 6. b; 7. a; 8. a

4. Time Line: A Short History of Tobacco and Cigarette Use

Least Recent—7 (1492); 2 (1560); 9 (ca. 1575); 4 (1613); 1 (1881); 6 (1899); 3 (1948); 8 (1955); 5 (1962)—Most Recent

5. Thoughts About Secondhand Smoke

Students need to understand that secondhand smoke is cigarette smoke inhaled by a person who is not directly inhaling it from a cigarette. Secondhand smoke is harmful because the smoke that person inhales still contains all of the chemicals that the smoker inhales. In fact, secondhand smoke is considered by some physicians to be more dangerous than smoke inhaled directly from a cigarette because it is unfiltered.

6. Young Kids and Smoking

Answers for the both parts will vary, but here are some sample answers: kids succumb to peer pressure; they see smoking on TV and imitate this; their parents smoke so they start because they admire their parents; they want to look cool; they want to rebel against authority.

7. Show Me the Money

  (a) Savings for one year: $1,825.00
  (b) The amount made on interest: $91.25
  (c) The interest plus the savings for 1 year: $1,916.25
  (d) Savings for 5 years: $9,581.25

(e) Savings for 10 years: $19,162.50

(f) Savings for 20 years: $38,325.00

(g) Savings for 40 years: $76,650.00

8. Getting Tough on Smoking: An Editorial

These are the three ideas that the author proposes to stop kids from smoking:

- Ban Hollywood from showing actors smoking on screen.
- Make people who are ill with smoking-related diseases pay all of their medical expenses.
- Send fourth and fifth graders on a mandatory class trip to a hospital to visit people who are dying from smoking-related illnesses.

11. Classifying the Types of Drugs

Stimulants	Depressants	Hallucinogens	Narcotics
cocaine	alcohol	LSD	codeine
caffeine	tranquilizers	PCP	morphine
nicotine	barbiturates	marijuana (can also go under various other categories as well)	heroin
crack			methadone

12. The Types-of-Drugs Chart

	Depressants	Hallucinogens	Narcotics	Stimulants
What this type of drug does	These are the opposite of stimulants. They act upon the central nervous system & slow down brain activity.	These drugs distort the user's senses and ability to perceive reality.	These drugs reduce pain and induce sleep.	These drugs act on the central nervous system & increase brain activity.
Examples of drugs in this category	alcohol tranquilizers barbiturates	LSD PCP	codeine morphine heroin methadone	cocaine caffeine nicotine crack
How the drugs enter the body	swallowed under tongue injection	swallowed injected smoked licked off paper chewed	injected snorted or sniffed smoked swallowed	swallowed snorted injected
Medical uses of this type of drug	to stop convulsions relief of tension to induce sleep	None	used for a pain relief	weight control to treat hyperactivity to treat narcolepsy

13. Facts or Myths on Drug Use

Fact: 2, 4, 5, 8, 9, 11, 14, 15, 16. *Myth:* 1, 3, 6, 7, 10, 12, 13

14. Time Line: History of Drug Regulations in the United States

Least Recent—4 (1890); 6 (1906); 3 (1914); 7 (1919); 1 (1938); 5 (1970); 2 (1988)—Most Recent

15. Drug Use and Different Ages

1. Ages 18 to 25 and 26 to 34.
2. Answers will vary. An acceptable answer would be that the people in these age groups are independent from their parents and therefore free to try drugs without upsetting parents. Also, these two groups are more likely to be in social environments where drugs are available.
3. Cocaine has the lowest percentage of use; alcohol has the highest.
4. Answers will vary. An acceptable answer would be that people are not likely to try cocaine because it is highly addictive and has the most negative side effects of the four drugs named. Tobacco and alcohol are also more popular because they are legal and easier to obtain.

16. The Drug-Use Continuum

Nonuser: Daoud; *experimental user:* Alexa; *occasional user:* Candace; *regular user:* Carlitos; *dependent user:* Oliver.

17. The Marijuana Expert

1. Marijuana is smoked in a pipe or a bong or is rolled in cigarette paper. It also may be used in a water pipe or vaporizer.
2. The reasons vary, but many teens start using marijuana because of peer pressure or because their friends use it.
3. The immediate effects are distorted perception, trouble concentrating and thinking, increased pulse rate, impaired coordination and memory, a feeling of relaxation, and increased sociability.
4. The long-term effects are changes in brain activity, breathing problems, weakened immune systems, cancer (some studies have proven this), personality changes, and possible heart and blood pressure problems.
5. A gateway drug is a drug that leads people to use more harmful drugs. Many crack and cocaine addicts started with marijuana.
6. Someone who has used marijuana is likely to have red eyes, act silly and giggly, have trouble doing simple things, feel hungry, and feel like talking a lot.
7. Answers will vary. Most will say their school counselor, a drug rehab center, a youth leader, and so on.

19. A Venn Diagram Comparing Tobacco and Marijuana

Answers will vary. Some similarities are that both can be smoked, both come from plants, and both have harmful effects. Some differences are that tobacco is legal while marijuana is not and that tobacco can be purchased in most variety and grocery stores while marijuana is not for sale in stores but is purchased from a dealer. Another difference is that people who buy tobacco pay a tax to the government; marijuana is not taxed by the government.

20. Caffeine

1. seven-ounce cup of automatic drip coffee (115-175 mg); 2. two-ounce serving of espresso (100 mg); 3. one can of Jolt cola (71 mg); 4. one 12-ounce glass of ice tea (70 mg); 5. one cup of imported, brewed tea (60 mg); 6. one can of Mountain Dew (55 mg); 7. one can of Coke or Diet Coke (46 mg); 8. one can of Dr. Pepper (40 mg); 9. one can of Pepsi (37 mg); 10. one Anacin tablet (32 mg); 11. one cup of hot cocoa (10 mg); 12. a one-ounce piece of milk chocolate (6 mg); 13. one cup of instant decaffeinated coffee (2-3 mg).

21. The Truth About Anabolic Steroids

True: 1, 2, 4, 6, 7, 9. *False:* 3, 5, 8

23. The Effects of Alcohol

Short-term effects: Slurs speech, impairs reflexes and reaction times, impairs judgment, relaxes the eye muscles making it difficult to focus, increases frequency of urination, causes nausea and vomiting, may cause anger, violence, or mood swings. *Long-term effects:* Causes liver damage; causes heart disease; causes irreversible brain or nerve damage; reduces production of sex hormones; causes cancer of the stomach; causes malnutrition; causes diseases of the stomach, digestive system, and pancreas; results in vitamin deficiency.

27. The Gray of Alcoholism

Students' definitions will vary. However, their definitions should express that alcoholics have difficulty controlling their drinking habits.

29. A Letter from a Child with FAS

1. Fetal alcohol syndrome occurs when women drink alcohol during their pregnancy. The alcohol enters the bloodstream where it passes through the placenta to the fetus in the womb. Some of the symptoms of FAS children are that they weigh less and are shorter than most infants, they may have heart abnormalities or other physical defects, and they have trouble concentrating and have short attention spans.
2. There is no cure for FAS.
3. Bobby wrote this letter to make pregnant women aware of FAS so they won't drink during their pregnancy.

31. Word Removal

Stay Clean Avoid Drugs

Section 2: Sex and Sex-Related Issues

33. Facts or Myths About Sex

Fact: 2, 7, 8, 9, 11, 12. *Myth:* 1, 3, 4, 5, 6, 10

35. Sexuality Throughout Our Lifetime

Early Childhood (birth to age 4)	- experience pleasure by touching their genitals - explore body parts - begin to develop a male or female identity - mimic adults - like to cuddle, hug, and kiss
Late Childhood (ages 5-8)	- continue to explore their bodies & experience pleasure from touching themselves - may become modest about their bodies - learn what is acceptable and not acceptable touching - have strong friendships, but don't understand or are aware of sexual desires
Pre-Adolescence (ages 9-13)	- begin to show signs of puberty & hormonal changes - may begin to masturbate - start developing crushes & becoming aware of the opposite sex - may begin to ask questions or wonder about sex - often still modest about their own bodies
Adolescence (ages 14-19)	- puberty changes continue - able to impregnate or become pregnant - may begin to date or develop intimate sexual relationships - begin to experiment & explore sexual possibilities - have strong sexual desires - may have sexual fantasies
EarlyAdulthood (ages 20-30)	- may experience pregnancy and childbirth - people vary — some are having first sexual encounters; some get married; some are still single - many are developing sexual relationships with a life partner
Adulthood (ages 31-60)	- many are continuing strong sexual relationships with a life partner - women go through menopause - some find their sexual desires slow down, but others find they're the same as in their early adulthood
Late Adulthood (61 plus)	- continue to have sexual desires & respond sexually but slowly - many experience isolation & loneliness due to loss of sexual partner - sexual intimacy may focus more on kissing & touching than on sex

36. The Four Phases of Sexual Intercourse

1. the excitement phase; 2. the plateau phase; 3. the orgasmic phase; 4. the resolution phase

37. Male versus Female

ovaries (F); testicles (M); prostate gland (M); fallopian tube (F); scrotum (M); clitoris (F); penis (M); seminal vesicle (M); cervix (F); epididymis (M); uterus (F); vagina (F); Cowper's glands (M); labia minora (F); vas deferens (M); labia majora (F); hymen (F); endometrium (F)

38. The Birth Control Chart

Type	Effective-ness	How it is obtained	Advantages	Disadvantages
Abstinence	100%	N/A	- 100% guarantee of unplanned pregnancies - helps eliminate a relationship that may only be based on sex	- there are no side effects
Birth Control Pills	99%	- prescribed by a family physician or gynecologist	- the woman does not have to rely on the man for birth control - it is highly effective in preventing pregnancy	- some side effects are weight gain & nausea - not good for smokers after age 35 - is not effective if a person forgets to take it - does not prevent STIs
The Latex Condom	85% higher if used with spermicide	- get at the drug store or supermarket	- easy to get - available at a low cost - highly effective in preventing both pregnancy & STIs	- if it breaks or comes off during sex it is ineffective - if used incorrectly it is also ineffective - some people find it takes away some sexual pleasure
Hormone Implants or Injections	99%	implanted in a woman's upper arm every 2 years or injected every 3 months by a physician	- highly effective in preventing pregnancies - may be used as a long-term method	- does not prevent STIs (sexually transmitted infections) - the initial cost is very expensive - some women get irregular periods
Diaphragm	85%	See a gynecologist or family physician	- the woman can determine the birth control	- does not prevent STIs (sexually transmitted infections) - can be awkward to insert and remove
IUD	97%	- implanted by a gynecologist or family physician	- very effective in preventing pregnancies - once it is inserted, a woman does not need to worry about it	- does not prevent STIs - can cause bleeding & cramps in a woman

39. Birth Control Crossword

Across: 4. abstinence; 6. Norplant™; 9. tubal ligation; 11. intercourse; 15. abortion; 17. semen; 18. nine; 20. morning after pill; 22. IUD. *Down:* 1. vasectomy; 2. pill; 3. vagina; 5. condom; 7. adoption; 8. withdrawal; 10. baby; 12. ejaculates; 13. contraception; 14. diaphragm; 16. spermicides; 19. egg; 21. penis

41. Dr. Birth Control

Answers will vary, but here are some suggestions:

1. *Recommended form of birth control*—Abstinence. *Reasons*—It is the only birth control method that is 100 percent effective; it is unlikely that this pair are emotionally mature enough for sex.

2. *Recommended form of birth control*—Hormonal contraceptives such as the pill or injections. *Reasons*—These methods are highly effective in preventing pregnancies.

3. *Recommended form of birth control*—Condoms as well as hormonal contraceptives for Kesha. *Reasons*—Condoms help prevent STIs; the hormonal contraceptives will help prevent pregnancies.

4. *Recommended form of birth control*—Any hormonal contraceptive. *Reasons*—They are very effective and safe.

42a. The Some-Thoughts-on-Abstinence Chart

Naneesh: Wants to wait until her wedding night because she wants this night to be special. *Mohammed:* Wants to wait until marriage because he does not want to worry about getting a girl pregnant or repeat his mom's experience. *Tina and John:* They felt that sex ruined their relationship because they became obsessed with sex and not each other. *Raneem:* She expects that once she has sex, every one of her relationships afterward will also involve sex; she doesn't want to ruin her reputation and she doesn't want to have too many partners before marriage. *Cassie:* She wants to wait for religious reasons.

44. Facts about Adoption

True: 1, 3, 4, 5, 7, 8, 9. *False:* 2, 6 (only 1 to 2 percent search for their birth parents), 10 (the number of couples is closer to one to two million)

45. What to Avoid During Pregnancy

Avoid: 1, 3, 4, 7, 8, 9, 11, 12, 13. *Okay:* 2, 5, 6, 10, 14

46. Stages in the Womb

1. fourth; 2. second; 3. first; 4. ninth; 5. sixth; 6. third

47. STI Unscramble

1. AIDS; 2. genital herpes; 3. syphilis; 4. gonorrhea; 5. chlamydia; 6. genital warts; 7. pubic lice; 8. hepatitis B

48. Dr. STI

1. The STI is AIDS. *Treatment:* There is no cure, but there are medications that can substantially prolong life.
2. The STI is herpes. *Treatment:* There is no cure, but medication can reduce the pain and soreness.
3. The STI is pubic lice. *Treatment:* Special medicated shampoo is available to get rid of the lice.

49. Ways of Acquiring HIV

No: 1, 3, 4, 6, 8, 9, 10, 13. *Yes:* 2, 5, 7, 11, 12, 14

52. Facts About Homosexuality

False: 1, 3, 4, 6, 7, 8. *True:* 2 (although the actual number may differ slightly, most studies prove that about 10 percent of the population is homosexual), 5

53. Options for Couples Who Want a Child

Artificial insemination: The woman is artificially inseminated with the sperm of her mate. *Artificial insemination by a donor:* The woman is artificially inseminated with a donor's sperm. *In vitro fertilization/embryo transfer:* An egg (or eggs) from the woman is combined with her mate's sperm, resulting in an embryo that is implanted into the woman. *In vitro fertilization with an egg donor:* A donor's eggs are combined with the sperm of the woman's mate; the resulting embryo is transferred into the woman to be carried to term.

55. Sexual Harassment Facts

1. False—Sexual harassment can happen to men and women.
2. False—No one deserves to be sexually harassed.
3. False—Yes, sexual comments can constitute sexual harassment.
4. True
5. False—There are lots of things people can do to stop sexual harassment. Most importantly, they should report what they consider to be sexual harassment even if they are not sure that the actions or words that make them feel uncomfortable constitute sexual harassment.

56. Sexual Harassment or Not Sexual Harassment?

Items 1, 4, 5, and 6 are definitely examples of sexual harassment because in all four of these cases, there is a person in a position of authority who is using sex (or suggestions of sex or sexual actions) as an abuse of power or a means of controlling an individual. *Item 2* is definitely not sexual harassment because the couple are equals. The comment may offend the girlfriend or excite her; in either case, it is not sexual harassment. *Item 3* probably should not be considered sexual harassment (although some students may argue that it is); in this case, the professor's comments are inappropriate but do not constitute sexual harassment.

57. Date Rape

What is date rape? It is the forcing of a woman to have sex by someone the woman knows. *Some ways women can avoid date rape are the following:* know as much about their date as possible; say what they mean; use body language that implies they are not interested in getting physical; do not lose control because of alcohol or drugs; always tell a friend or someone they know where they are going on their date; avoid men who are jealous and heavy drinkers; learn how to defend themselves.

58. Date-Rape Decisions

For Situation I, emphasize to students that Carol's making up a story is not only extremely wrong but is considered a criminal offense. *For Situations II and III,* it is important to explain to boys especially that when a girl says no, she always means no.

61. Sex Jeopardy

Saying No to Pregnancy—100: birth control pill; *200:* condom; *300:* abstinence; *400:* the diaphragm or the female condom; *500:* IUD

The ABCs of STIs—100: AIDS, HIV, hepatitis B and C; *200:* pubic lice; *300:* genital warts; *400:* herpes; *500:* chlamydia

She Parts—100: egg; *200:* vagina; *300:* ovaries; *400:* fallopian tubes; *500:* uterus

He Parts—100: sperm; *200:* penis; *300:* testes or testicles; *400:* urethra; *500:* scrotum

Talk the Talk—100: female; *200:* sexually transmitted infection; *300:* testosterone; *400:* menstruation; *500:* nocturnal emissions

62. It Takes Three

Parts of the female sexual anatomy: fallopian tube, ovary, uterus

Parts of the male sexual anatomy: scrotum, epididymis, penis

Birth control that is used only during sex: diaphragm, condom, sponge

Male and female hormones: estrogen, progesterone, testosterone

Stages of development in the womb: placenta, embryo, fetus

Chemical birth control: birth control pill, Norplant™, spermicide

Methods of sex that can spread HIV: oral, anal, vaginal

Sexual problems: premature ejaculation, impotence, vaginismus

STDs that begin with the letter G: genital herpes, genital warts, gonorrhea

STDs: syphilis, AIDS, chlamydia

63. Alphabet Soup

V	W	U	D	I	*P*	*E*	*N*	*I*	*S*	R
P	E	N	O	V	*K*	*I*	*S*	*S*	*E*	*S*
W	O	M	I	*H*	*Y*	*M*	*E*	*N*	O	R
F	E	T	*V*	*A*	*G*	*I*	*N*	*A*	U	S
O	*P*	*R*	*E*	*G*	*N*	*A*	*N*	*T*	A	C
P	I	L	M	A	*C*	*O*	*N*	*D*	*O*	*M*
K	*W*	*I*	*T*	*H*	*D*	*R*	*A*	*W*	*A*	*L*
O	V	D	*T*	*E*	*S*	*T*	*E*	*S*	T	E
J	A	M	T	C	*W*	*A*	*R*	*T*	*S*	L
M	E	N	*C*	*E*	*R*	*V*	*I*	*X*	Y	Z
L	O	V	E	I	*F*	*E*	*T*	*U*	*S*	S
I	*U*	*T*	*E*	*R*	*U*	*S*	W	O	M	D
B	L	M	N	*L*	*A*	*B*	*I*	*A*	O	P
C	A	N	Y	O	*Z*	*Y*	*G*	*O*	*T*	*E*
A	V	W	*S*	*E*	*X*	*U*	*A*	*L*	T	M
S	*S*	*P*	*E*	*R*	*M*	E	I	V	H	T
C	*O*	*N*	*S*	*E*	*Q*	*U*	*E*	*N*	*C*	*E*
R	*S*	*C*	*R*	*O*	*T*	*U*	*M*	D	F	H
B	O	X	E	L	*J*	*E*	*L*	*L*	*Y*	Z
S	*F*	*E*	*R*	*T*	*I*	*L*	*E*	V	I	R
K	J	S	*E*	*M*	*B*	*R*	*Y*	*O*	D	G
B	*C*	*L*	*I*	*T*	*O*	*R*	*I*	*S*	M	S
E	*N*	*O*	*R*	*P*	*L*	*A*	*N*	*T*	W	E
E	*D*	*I*	*A*	*P*	*H*	*R*	*A*	*G*	*M*	T
F	I	X	O	*O*	*V*	*U*	*L*	*A*	*T*	*E*
G	*P*	*L*	*A*	*C*	*E*	*N*	*T*	*A*	H	I

Section 3: Love, Relationships, Marriage, and Family

68. All About Cliques
Clique: 1, 3, 4, 7. *Positive group:* 2, 5, and 6

69. Break the Clique
In Scenario 1, recommend to your students that they should find a friend who will work with them to include the shunned student. It is sometimes unwise for a student to act alone in trying to befriend another because a group may turn against an individual; they are not as likely to turn against two or three people. Also worth mentioning to your students here is that in a team sport, in particular, the team will never succeed if the group focuses on individuals rather than on playing as a unit. *In Scenario 2,* stress that students should try to put themselves in other people's shoes. Many people arrive in America from horrific situations; we need to welcome all newcomers and treat them with kindness and respect.

74. Is It Love or Infatuation?
Love: 1, 4, 5, 7, 9, 10, 12. *Infatuation:* 2, 3, 6, 8, 11

76. Sternberg's Love Triangle Theory: Worksheet 1
The definitions will vary, but for the purpose of this exercise here are the types of definitions you should look for: *passion*—strong emotion and enthusiasm for the other person (may also include sexual desire); *intimacy*—intimate knowledge of another person's thoughts, desires, passions, and needs; *commitment*—dedication to the relationship.

78. Sternberg's Love Triangle Theory: Worksheet 3
1. companionate; 2. infatuation; 3. empty; 4. romantic; 5. liking; 6. fatuous; 7. nonlove; 8. consummate

88. Can These Marriages Be Saved?
Here are some points to share with your students during a class discussion.

> *Scenario I:* In today's world, both men and women need to help with child care. It is no longer acceptable for men to avoid helping raise their children.

> *Scenario II:* It is extremely important for couples to communicate about what they want in a marital relationship before they get married.

> *Scenario III:* Money and how it is handled causes a lot of problems for couples. Couples should communicate and agree about spending habits before marriage.

94. Who's in What Stage of the Family Life Cycle?
1. starting family; 2. post-parenting couples; 3. aging couples; 4. families with preteens; 5. newly married; 6. families with preschool children; 7. families with young adults; 8. families with teens

Section 4: Life Skills

95. Maslow's Hierarchy of Needs

1. self-worth needs; 2. love and friendship needs; 3. physical needs; 4. safety needs; 5. self-fulfillment needs

98. High and Low Self-Esteem

Low: 1, 4, 6, 7, 10, 12. *High:* 2, 3, 5, 8, 9, 11

101. Learning Assertiveness

The definitions for passive, aggressive, and assertive will vary, but here are some sample definitions: *passive*—being submissive and offering no opposition; *aggressive*—being openly hostile and forceful; *assertive*—tending to assert oneself in a positive manner.

Answers to statements: 1. aggressive; 2. assertive; 3. passive; 4. passive; 5. aggressive; 6. assertive

102. More on Assertiveness

Assertive reactions: You look the person directly in the eyes. You acknowledge the other person's feelings but also offer an explanation for your own feelings. You make sure your voice is strong with a confident tone. You make sure that your facial expressions always match what you're saying. You use "I" statements whenever possible. You are confident in what you are saying and aren't afraid to take a stand.

Aggressive reactions: You raise your voice and yell at the person. You use sarcasm and put-downs. You stand as close as possible to the person you are addressing.

Passive reactions: You whisper or mumble. You show that you are embarrassed or uncomfortable whenever someone compliments you. You apologize even if you didn't do anything wrong.

104. Conflict Outcomes

1. collaborative problem solving; 2. avoidance; 3. passivity and dominance; 4. compromise

109. Name That Communication Blocker

1. ridiculing; 2. preaching; 3. blaming; 4. ordering; 5. diverting; 6. blaming; 7. ridiculing; 8. diverting; 9. ordering; 10. preaching

120. Types of Violence

Answers will vary, but here are some sample definitions: *bullying*—repeated attacks on others done by an individual or group; *psychological violence*—mental intimidation; *sexual violence*—rape or unwanted sexual touching; *physical violence*—anything involving hitting or physically harming the other person

123. Advice in Code

Coded message: Don't be afraid to be yourself and follow your own path in life.

Section 5: Stress

126. What Is Their Life Change Index?

1. 140; 2. 310; 3. 130; 4. 170; 5. 180; 6. 83

133. Sources-of-Stress Game

A1: becoming overweight; **A2:** feeling down; **A3:** overworked and underpaid; **A4:** increasing responsibility; **B1:** little hope for the future; **B2:** getting knocked up (pregnant); **B3:** stress in school; **B4:** a separated family; **C1:** a broken heart; **C2:** a decreasing bank balance; **C3:** falling grades; **C4:** no friends; **D1:** a death in the family; **D2:** mood swings; **D3:** low SAT scores; **D4:** a change in residence

134. The Four Stages of Stress

1. resistance; 2. alarm; 3. exhaustion; 4. adaptation

135. Fight or Flight

Fight: 3, 7. *Flight:* 1, 2, 4, 5, 6, 8

141. How Can You Help Your Stressed Friend?

Students' answers will vary. However, it is important for students to note that both of these friends need professional help. Sometimes students try to help people who should really see a professional. The object of this worksheet is to stress to students that while sometimes they can support a friend, the friend may also require the support of a professional.

142. A Suicide Awareness Quiz

True: 3, 5. *False:* 1, 2, 4, 6, 7, 8, 9

143. Dealing with a Grieving Friend

Do: 3, 4, 5, 8, 10. *Don't:* 1, 2, 6, 7, 9

146. Which Stage of Grief (in Dying Patients)?

1. anger; 2. acceptance; 3. bargaining; 4. denial and isolation; 5. depression

Section 6: Food and Food-Related Issues

151. A Food Pyramid Puzzle

Fats, oils, and sweets group: use sparingly; *milk, yogurt, and cheese group:* 2-3 servings; *meat, poultry, dry beans, eggs, and nuts group:* 2-3 servings; *vegetable group:* 3-5 servings; *fruit group:* 2-4 servings; *bread, cereal, pasta, and rice group:* 6-11 servings

155. Calorie Calculations

Meal 1: 390 calories; *Meal 2:* 831 calories; *Meal 3:* 1,358 calories; *Meal 4:* 654 calories

156. What to Know About H₂O

1. nutrient; 2. two-thirds; 3. water; 4. two to three quarts; 5. dehydrated; 6. juice; 7. caffeine; 8. six to eight

157. Let's Learn About Vitamins

1. c; 2. a; 3. c; 4. b; 5. c; 6. d

158. Cholesterol: Fact or Fiction

1. fact; 2. fiction (the oxygen and hydrogen makeup of fat and cholesterol is different); 3. fact; 4. fact; 5. fiction (lipoproteins are produced in the liver); 6. fiction (it is actually high-density lipoprotein [HDL] cholesterol that carries away low-density lipoprotein [LDL] cholesterol); 7. fiction (this is actually describing low-density lipoproteins, not high-density lipoproteins); 8. fact; 9. fact; 10. fact

159. Protein Fill-in-the-Blanks

People need protein for many reasons. For example, protein is a source of *energy*. It is necessary for *growth* and the repair of *tissues*. Protein also helps transport *oxygen* and nutrients throughout the body. Protein is needed for every *cell* of our body, and it is made up of *amino acids*. There are *22* different amino acids, and the various types found in protein determine its *biological* activity. Our bodies *manufacture* 13 of the amino acids, but not the other *nine*. Since we need those nine amino acids in order to function, *protein* is very important in our diets. Many *animal* products are good sources of protein; for example, poultry, eggs, milk, fish, meat, and *cheese*. Other sources of protein are peanut butter, *rice,* beans, seeds, *nuts,* and grains. People need to get *10 to 12* percent of their calories from protein.

160. All You Ever Wanted to Know About Fiber

The foods that provide us with fiber are bran cereals, whole-grain bread, popcorn, apples, strawberries, corn, carrots, figs, white potatoes, oranges, oatmeal, and turnips.

162. Fat Classification

Butter: S; *sunflower seeds:* P; *chocolate cake:* S; *potato chips:* S; *canola oil:* M; *French fries:* S; *olives:* M; *cream:* S; *walnuts:* P; *cheese:* S; *peanut oil:* M; *soybean oil:* P.

163. Fat Reduction

These are the items that are lower in fat: one glass of skim milk, quarter-cup of grated mozzarella cheese, four ounces chicken with no skin, a ham sandwich with mustard, half-cup of unbuttered popcorn, one pear, one bran muffin, one piece of apple crisp, quarter-cup of creamed cottage cheese, one boiled or poached egg, and one tuna sandwich.

164. Crazy About Carbohydrates

Yes: 1, 2, 5, 6, 7, 11. *No:* 3 (change the word *helium* to *oxygen*); 4 (change the word *inactive* to *active*); 8 (change the word *complex* to *simple*); 9 (change the word *simple* to *complex*); 10 (this should read: Carbohydrates that are not used will be converted into fats.)

165. Our Addiction to Additives

Answers will vary, but here are some sample answers: *Advantages:* additives make food taste better; they preserve food, preventing them from spoiling easily; they lower production costs; they make cooking more convenient; they protect consumers from food-related diseases (like hepatitis); they allow for greater profits for the food industry; they allow the food industry to control the quality of the product more easily. *Disadvantages:* not all additives are necessary, and they don't always offer nutritional value; consumption of some additives may lead to health problems (such as cancer); many additives are used to make the food "look better" but by doing this may decrease the nutritional value; processed foods with additives cost consumers more money.

166. Food Categories

Answers will vary, but here are some sample answers: *carbohydrates*—pasta, bread, asparagus, beans, banana, rice, honey; *protein*—meat, peanut butter, beans, eggs, milk, poultry, fish, cheese; *fiber*—figs, apples, popcorn, bran cereals, carrots, turnips, whole-grain bread; *polyunsaturated fats*—walnuts, soybean oil, sunflower seeds, fish, almonds, sesame oil, liquid or soft margarine

167. Just Because It's a Salad Doesn't Mean It's Healthy

Answers will vary, but here are some sample answers.

Caesar salad: *What makes this salad unhealthy?* The salad dressing, bacon bits, and croutons are high in fat. *How to make the recipe healthier?* Don't add the bacon bits or croutons and use lowfat mayonnaise in the dressing. Also, put less dressing on the salad.

Broccoli salad: *What makes this salad unhealthy?* The bacon and cheese are high in fat, along with the mayonnaise in the dressing. And naturally, sugar isn't great either. *How to make the recipe healthier?* Use lowfat mayonnaise and substitute something like sunflower seeds for the bacon. Also, use lowfat cheese.

Five-Cup Salad: *What makes this salad unhealthy?* Everything! *How to make the recipe healthier?* Add various fresh fruits (such as blueberries, fresh pineapple, or mango), use plain yogurt instead of sour cream (or go half and half), sprinkle only a little unsweetened coconut and marshmallows on top.

168. Can You Help These Eaters?

Answers will vary, but here are some sample answers: *Person 1*—needs to cut down on his or her fat intake. He or she needs to eat healthier meals. *Person 2*—is not getting enough nutrients and needs to eat more. (Missing meals is not healthy.) *Person 3*—needs to make some healthier food choices, particularly at dinnertime.

169. An Eating Disorder True-False Quiz

True: 1, 5, 6, 7, 9. *False:* 2, 3, 4, 8

170. Name That Disorder

I. anorexia; II. bulimia; III. compulsive eating. (Please note: When making the suggestions for how each person can overcome his or her disorder, students should emphasize in all three cases that the person should seek professional help.)

172. The Do's and Don'ts of Helping Someone with an Eating Disorder

1. don't; 2. do; 3. don't; 4. do; 5. don't; 6. don't; 7. do; 8. do; 9. do; 10. do

173. The Food Vocabulary Word Game

1. nutrient; 2. calcium; 3. nutritionist; 4. carbohydrate; 5. sugar; 6. vegetarian; 7. bulimia; 8. calorie; 9. anorexia; 10. caffeine; 11. monounsaturated fat; 12. minerals; 13. protein; 14. fats; 15. starch; 16. vitamins; 17. water

Message: Eat three balanced meals a day!

Section 7: Your Body and Body Image

178. Cosmetic Plastic Surgery

1. c; 2. c; 3. a; 4. b

179. Body-Parts Connections

Bladder—storage tank for urine; *small intestine*—main site for absorption of food; *kidneys*—filter waste products from the blood; *heart*—the muscle that pumps blood from veins through arteries; *stomach*—where food goes after it is swallowed and where it is partly digested; *brain*—controls the body's processes, the center of thought and memory; *lungs*—where the exchange of oxygen and carbon dioxide takes place; *large intestine*—where water is absorbed from digested food; *liver*—cleans waste and harmful chemicals from the blood and processes food into usable products.

180. Body-Parts Vocabulary

Ear: cochlea; *female breast:* milk duct; *heart:* right atrium; *eye:* retina; *brain:* frontal lobe; *arm:* biceps; *mouth:* salivary glands; *foot:* metatarsals; *hand:* metacarpals

181. Muscle Word Search

1. hamstring; 2. gluteus maximus; 3. gastrocnemius; 4. rectus abdominis; 5. temporalis; 6. biceps; 7. triceps; 8. soleus; 9. external oblique; 10. quadriceps; 11. trapezius; 12. pectoralis

G	L	U	T	E	U	S	M	A	X	I	M	U	S	G	L	P
L	N	X	L	O	S	O	L	E	U	S	W	A	U	C	X	E
U	T	I	T	X	T	P	U	V	W	E	K	B	I	V	W	C
T	R	A	R	O	S	U	E	I	F	J	D	F	M	V	A	T
S	A	P	I	T	L	Z	V	C	R	S	I	S	E	T	U	O
P	M	A	C	B	S	Q	O	G	I	Y	C	H	N	N	L	R
E	O	A	E	E	N	M	L	L	C	B	A	X	C	G	K	A
C	V	D	P	L	M	I	A	D	K	Q	U	A	O	T	R	L
I	I	B	S	B	R	R	C	H	E	R	E	F	R	O	S	I
R	U	R	Q	D	O	F	P	W	D	L	R	M	T	U	M	S
D	T	R	A	P	E	Z	I	U	S	Q	U	V	S	S	X	T
A	H	A	M	K	G	H	N	O	W	I	J	S	A	R	K	B
U	V	E	I	U	M	V	T	J	N	P	Z	O	G	L	A	Y
Q	T	E	X	T	E	R	N	A	L	O	B	L	I	Q	U	E
S	I	N	I	M	O	D	B	A	S	U	T	C	E	R	K	Q

182. Right Muscle, Right Exercise

Triceps: partial sit-up; *quadriceps:* concentration curl; *abdominals:* preacher curl; *deltoids:* lunge; *pectorals:* lunge; *erectors:* dumbbell press; *latissimus dorsi:* squat; *gluteals:* preacher curl

183. The Human Skeleton Crossword

Across: 3. ulna; 5. clavicle; 7. vertebrae; 9. tibia; 10. tendons; 12. tarsals; 13. skeleton; 16. metatarsals; 17. mandible; 18. patella; 19. femur; 20. pelvis. *Down:* 1. ligaments; 2. humerus; 4. metacarpals; 5. cartilage; 6. cranium; 8. phalange; 11. joint; 13. sternum; 14. carpals; 15. ribs

184. Female Reproductive System Vocabulary

1. mons pubis; 2. vaginal opening; 3. cervix; 4. fallopian tubes; 5. uterus; 6. ovaries; 7. clitoris; 8. hymen; 9. labia (inner and outer)

185. Male Reproductive System Vocabulary

1. vas deferens; 2. penis; 3. prostate gland; 4. urethra; 5. testicles; 6. seminal vesicles; 7. epididymis; 8. Cowper's glands; 9. scrotum

186. The Respiratory System Matching Exercise

Alveoli: 8; *bronchi:* 7; *carbon dioxide:* 4; *lungs:* 9; *nose (and nasal cavity):* 3; *oxygen:* 1; *pharynx:* 5; *pulmonary veins:* 10; *respiratory system:* 2; *trachea:* 6.

187. The Digestion Puzzle

7. The food leaves the stomach a bit at a time; *4.* The tongue helps push the food to the back of the mouth so it can move into the esophagus; *1.* Food enters the mouth; *8.* The food enters the small intestine, where the digestive juices finish breaking down the food; *3.* During chewing, saliva is squirted into the mouth to help soften the food; *9.* Food waste goes to the large intestines where it forms feces; *2.* Teeth begin to break down the food; *6.* The food moves from the esophagus into the stomach, where the food mixes with acids from the stomach; *5.* The chewed food is swallowed and travels down the esophagus.

189. Genetics and Your Health

You may wish to follow this activity with a discussion. Ask students why it is important to know about their parents' health. What does it mean to how they live their lives, for instance, if their dad suffered a heart attack at age 45 or if their mom is subject to migraines?

190. Dr. Doctor's Magic Square

a	16	b	2	c	3	d	13
e	5	f	11	g	10	h	8
i	9	j	7	k	6	l	12
m	4	n	14	o	15	p	1

The magic number is 34.

191. What Makes You Ill?

Bacteria: scarlet fever, salmonella food poisoning, whooping cough, cholera. *Virus:* common cold, flu, measles, mumps, smallpox, AIDS

192. Five Diseases and Conditions That May Affect Teens

Disease	Definition	Cause	Symptom	Treatment
Asthma (1)	This is a life-threatening ... sugar into useable energy. **2. Diabetes**	There is no single ... lack of sleep, & low sugar levels. **3. Epilepsy**	Symptoms vary from ... like blindness or memory loss, etc. **4. Lyme**	This disease can be treated through antibiotics. **4. Lyme**
Diabetes (2)	this is a condition ... sudden attacks or seizures. **3. Epilepsy**	This is not passed as ... passed through kissing. **5. Mono**	Symptoms may vary ... dry cough & wheezing. **1. Asthma**	Although this condition ... anticonvulsant medication. **3. Epilepsy**
Epilepsy (3)	This disease affects ... resulting in breathing difficulties. **1. Asthma**	Bacteria transmitted ... infected deer tick cause the disease. **4. Lyme**	Fatigue is the most significant ... enlarged spleen. **5. Mono**	People with type 1 ... altering diet and oral medication **2. Diabetes**
Lyme Disease (4)	This is an infection ... Epstein-Barr virus. **5. Mono**	Physical activity ... attack or reaction. **1. Asthma**	Some people may ... blurred vision. **2. Diabetes**	It cannot be cured ... about a month. **5. Mono**
Monoucleosis (5)	This bacterial disease ... northeast States. **4. Lyme**	The cause is ... aging are significant factors **2. Diabetes**	Seizures are the ... symptom. **3. Epilepsy**	There is no cure ... control an attack. **1. Asthma**

193. Basic First-Aid Crossword

Across: 2. shock; 6. dehydrated; 8. sprains; 9. nonpoisonous; 10. back; 13. resuscitation; 15. compound; 16. flies. *Down:* 1. stinger; 3. hypothermia; 4. clean; 5. wounds; 6. dislocation; 7. hands; 11. mosquitoes; 12. Band-Aids™; 14. closed

194. Diagnose the Emergency

Person A: *What is the problem?* The person is choking. *How can you help this person?* 1. Stand behind the victim; 2. wrap arms around victim's waist; 3. place thumb side of fist against middle of victim's abdomen, just above navel; 4. grasp fist with other hand; 5. give quick upward thrusts; 6. repeat until object is coughed up or person becomes unconscious. **Person B:** *What is the problem?* The person has a bee sting. *How can you help this person?* 1. Remove the stinger; 2. wash wound; 3. cover; 4. apply a cold pack; 5. watch for signs of an allergic reaction. **Person C:** *What is the problem?* The person has heat stroke. *How can you help this person?* 1. Remove the person to a cooler place—for example, the shade of a tree; 2. keep the person lying down; 3. cool the body any way possible—for example, put ice on the person, pour water on him, and so on; 4. provide the person with plenty of cool liquids.

195. Preventing Cardiovascular Disease

Controllable: insufficient exercise, stress (although some stress is uncontrollable), smoking, poor eating habits, being overweight, drinking too much alcohol, having high blood pressure. *Uncontrollable:* gender, increasing age, family history of cardiovascular disease

197. Components of Fitness

1. c; 2. a; 3. a; 4. b

198. Anaerobic Energy, Aerobic Energy, and DOM

1. anaerobic; 2. aerobic; 3. anaerobic; 4. anaerobic; 5. aerobic. *Three ways to prevent DOM are:* start a regular exercise routine and build up gradually; exercise regularly; stretch before and after exercising.

BIBLIOGRAPHY

American Lung Association. "The Human Respiratory System." [www.lungusa.org]. Aug. 2001.

American Lung Association. "Fact Sheet: Smoking." [www.lungusa.org]. June 2002.

American Society of Aesthetic Plastic Surgery. "ASAP's 2000 Statistics on Cosmetic Surgery." [http://surgery.org/pdf_files/2000stats.pdf]. 2001.

Bartleby Quotations. [www.bartleby.com/quotations]. 2000.

Bodywise. "Facts About Eating Disorders." [www.girlpower.gov/girlarea/bodywise/index.htm]. 2003.

Bohmer, D. "The Top Ten Sources of Stress for Kids." Mind/Body/Medical Institute. [http://www.familyeducation.com]. 1998.

Cheal, D. *Family and the State of Theory.* Toronto: University of Toronto Press, 1991.

Cohen, J. M., and Cohen, M. J. (eds.). *The New Penguin Dictionary of Quotations.* New York: Penguin Books, 1992.

Dodds de Wolf, G., Gregg, R., Harris, B., and Scargill, M. *Gage Canadian Dictionary.* Toronto: Gage Educational Publishing, 1998.

Donaldio, S., and Smith, J. (eds.). *The New York Public Library Book of 20th Century American Quotations.* New York: Stonesong Press, 1992.

Eichler, M. *Family Shifts.* New York: Oxford University Press, 1997.

Engel, J. *Handwriting Analysis Self-Taught.* New York: Elsevier/Nelson, 1980.

Fienden, M. *The Calorie Factor: The Dieter's Companion.* New York: Simon & Schuster, 1989.

Goldman, J. L. (ed.). *Webster's New World Dictionary.* Cleveland, Ohio: Modern Curriculum Press, 1993.

Goodman, R. *A Quick Guide to Food Safety.* San Diego: Silvercat Publications, 1992.

Grade 6: Health and Physical Education. Ontario: Ontario Physical and Health Education Association, 2000.

Grade 7: Health and Physical Education. Ontario: Ontario Physical and Health Education Association, 2000.

Grade 8: Health and Physical Education. Ontario: Ontario Physical and Health Education Association, 2000.

Grade 9: Health and Physical Education. Ontario: Ontario Physical and Health Education Association, 2000.

Grade 10: Health and Physical Education. Ontario: Ontario Physical and Health Education Association, 2000.

Healthy Weights: A New Way of Looking at Your Weight and Height. Ontario: Ontario Ministry of Health, 1991.

Julien, R. M. *A Primer of Drug Action* (7th ed.). New York: Freeman, 1996.

Kubler-Ross, E. *Living with Death and Dying.* New York: Collier Books, 1982.

Kubler-Ross, E. *On Death and Dying.* New York: Macmillan, 1991.

Macmillan Health Encyclopedia #1: Body Systems. New York: Macmillan, 1999.

Macmillan Health Encyclopedia #2: Communicable Diseases. New York: Macmillan, 1999.

Macmillan Health Encyclopedia #3: Noncommunicable Diseases and Disorders. New York: Macmillan, 1999.

Macmillan Health Encyclopedia #4: Nutrition and Fitness. New York: Macmillan, 1999.

Macmillan Health Encyclopedia #6: Sexuality and Reproduction. New York: Macmillan, 1999.

Macmillan Health Encyclopedia #7: Drugs, Alcohol, and Tobacco. New York: Macmillan, 1999.

Maisto, S., Galizio, M., and Connors, G. J. *Drug Use and Abuse* (3rd ed.). Orlando, Fla.: Harcourt Brace, 1999.

Martens Miller, P. *Sex Is Not a Four-Letter Word.* New York: Crossroad, 1994.

Maslow, A. *Motivation and Personality* (3rd ed.). New York: HarperCollins, 1987.

McRae, R. "Top Ten Pieces of Advice to Live By." Unpublished manuscript, James McQueen Public School, Guelph, Ontario, Canada.

National Council for Adoption. "Adoption Facts, 2000." [www.ncfa-usa.org]. 2000.

Ray, O., and Ksir, C. *Drugs, Society, and Human Behavior* (8th ed.). New York: McGraw-Hill, 1999.

Richardson, R., and Richardson, L. *Birth Order and You.* Bellingham, Wash.: Self-Council Press, 1990.

Rizzo Toner, P. *Diet and Nutrition Activities.* Paramus, N.J.: Center for Applied Research in Education, 1993.

Rizzo Toner, P. *Relationships and Communication Activities.* Paramus, N.J.: Center for Applied Research in Education, 1993.

Rizzo Toner, P. *Sex Education Activities.* Paramus, N.J.: Center for Applied Research in Education, 1993.

Rizzo Toner, P. *Stress-Management and Self-Esteem Activities.* Paramus, N.J.: Center for Applied Research in Education, 1993.

Rizzo Toner, P. *Substance Abuse Prevention Activities.* Paramus, N.J.: Center for Applied Research in Education, 1993.

Rizzo Toner, P., and Milliken, M. D. *The Health Teacher's Book of Lists.* Hoboken, N.J.: John Wiley & Sons, 1999.

Ronzio, R. A. *The Encyclopedia of Nutrition and Good Health.* New York: Facts on File, 1997.

Shea, C. H., and Wright, D. L. *An Introduction to Human Movement: The Science of Physical Education.* Needham Heights, Mass.: Allyn and Bacon, 1997.

Sher, B. *Live the Life You Love.* New York: Dell, 1996.

Sizer, F., and Whitney, E. *Nutrition: Concepts and Controversies* (8th ed.). Belmont, Calif.: Wadsworth/Thomson Learning, 2000.

Sternberg, R. *The Triangle of Love: Intimacy, Passion, Commitment.* New York: Basic Books, 1988.

Theodore, A. *The Origins and Sources of Drugs.* Broomall, Penn.: Chelsea House Publishers, 1988.

Lightning Source UK Ltd.
Milton Keynes UK
UKHW03f0751231018
331024UK00005B/44/P